THAILAND
TODAY

THAILAND TODAY
A Visit to Modern Siam

VALENTIN CHU

THOMAS Y. CROWELL COMPANY

NEW YORK • ESTABLISHED 1834

Contents

THAILAND

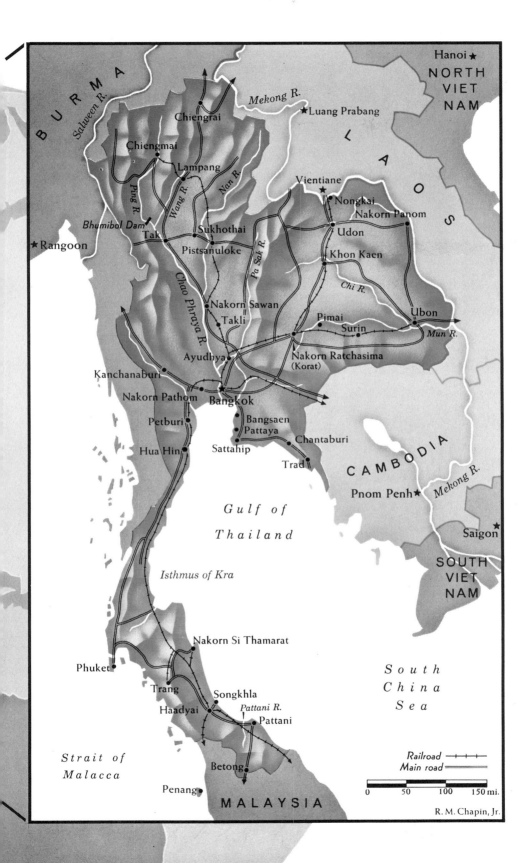

BURMA

Salween R.

Mekong R.

Hanoi ★

NORTH
VIET
NAM

Chiengrai

★ Luang Prabang

L
A
O
S

Chiengmai

Lampang

Ping R.

Wang R.

Nan R.

Vientiane ★

Nongkai

Nakorn Panom

Bhumibol Dam

Tak

Sukhothai

Udon

★ Rangoon

Pistsanuloke

Pa Sak R.

Khon Kaen

Chao Phraya R.

Chi R.

Nakorn Sawan

Takli

Pimai

Surin

Ubon

Mun R.

Ayudhya

Nakorn Ratchasima
(Korat)

Kanchanaburi

Nakorn Pathom

Bangkok

Petburi

Bangsaen
Pattaya

Sattahip

Chantaburi

Hua Hin

Trad

CAMBODIA

Pnom Penh ★

Mekong R.

Gulf of

Thailand

Saigon ★

SOUTH
VIET
NAM

Isthmus of Kra

South

China

Sea

Nakorn Si Thamarat

Phuket

Trang

Songkhla

Haadyai

Pattani R.

Pattani

Strait of
Malacca

Betong

Penang

MALAYSIA

Railroad +—+—+
Main road ═══

0   50   100   150 mi.

R. M. Chapin, Jr.

A Smiling Country

PASSENGERS who climb down from the big transport planes at Bangkok's Don Muang Airport soon sense the feeling of well-being that seems to permeate the atmosphere of Thailand. Noted by many journalists and other commentators, it might be described as a general satisfaction with the human condition.

American travel writer Myra Waldo has observed that in reading tourist folders about Thailand it is impossible to avoid running across the assertion that the Thais are a "smiling" people. "Peculiarly enough," writes Miss Waldo (in her *Travel Guide to the Orient and Pacific*), "although most tourist folders are pure nonsense, this happens to be an absolutely true statement." In Thailand, it appears, almost everybody smiles almost all of the time. Partly this is a result of natural amiability, of a traditional habit of thinking which gives value to harmony and the smoothing of social relations rather than the combativeness that so often wins success in Western society. If forced into out-right disagreement with another, the Thai will make his position known by polite hints and discreet signals of dissent — smiling all the while as if there were no disagreement at all. This oblique method of conduct is often baffling to hard-driving American executives doing business in Thailand.

Another reason for the characteristically sunny outlook of the Thai people is an historic freedom from exploitation. Unique among the countries of Southeast Asia, Thailand was never colonized by Europeans in the era when empire-building was in fashion. Thus, Western visitors to Thailand today encounter none of the resentment and racial antagonism that might be experienced in, say, Burma or Indonesia. And huge numbers of Westerners are now making Bangkok a stopover in their world travels, coming away with impressions of an alluring country and a friendly, happy people. The general state of euphoria in Thailand has been heightened for some years past by a booming prosperity. Thai currency is the hardest in South-east Asia. And a large number of government development plans are impelling the nation toward modernization in the Western sense — a modernization which includes a wider distribution of consumer goods to the Thai people.

The country was called Siam until 1939, and some of its indigenous products will no doubt always be known by the appellation "Siamese" — as in the case of Siamese cats. But this land of the Thai people, a remarkably homogeneous racial grouping of very early origin, is now properly re-ferred to as Thailand (pronounced "Tieland"). The change of name — and the changes brought about in recent years by economic development and modernization — have not altered the essential character of the country. Thailand is a bright mosaic of green jungles and brown canals, of iridescent temples sparkling in the sun, and teakwood houses with leaning walls that stand on stilts like drunken bugs on wobbly legs.

Thailand is also the tinkle of temple bells, the quicksilver voices of lovely women in shocking-pink silk, the clip-clop of wooden sandals, the wail of itinerant noodle hawkers, and the creaking of bullock carts. These ancient and — to a Western ear — romantic Oriental sounds may be overlaid now and again with the screech of city traffic or the roar of jet aircraft — just as gilded temple spires may be obscured here and there by concrete buildings and neon signs. But Thailand is still the Far East; and to reinforce visual and aural impressions there are the timeless Far Eastern smells of salted fish, fried chili, baked banana, cinnamon, garlic, canal silt, humanity in sweat, jasmine, turmeric, sandalwood and incense.

History has left many noteworthy relics in Thailand. At Kanchanaburi are Neolithic burial sites, and not far away is the cemetery where rest the Allied soldiers of World War II who perished in building the "Death Railway" across the Bridge on the River Kwai. The ruins of Pimai, which include majestic towers and elaborately carved stone galleries, bespeak the lost splendor of the Khmers, once the occupants of this country, who built Pimai a hundred years before they built Angkor Wat. Tucked away in a forgotten, teak-fringed valley is Sukhothai, the 13th Century capital of the Thai people, where crumbling edifices echo the Golden Age of Siamese art. Farther south are the jungle-covered ruins of Ayudhya, capital of Thailand for four centuries until razed by the Burmese in 1767, once a city bigger and more splendid than London.

11

Today, sprawling massively along the Chao Phraya River, at the head of the delta where the great waterway empties into the Gulf of Thailand, is the contemporary capital of Bangkok, the largest city of Southeast Asia and a transportation hub from which radiate air routes to all the major points on this section of the globe.

In the past two centuries, Bangkok has seen many visitors from distant places arrive by square-rigged sailing ship, Arab dhow, dragon-eyed junk, European gunboat, tramp steamer and — most often today — by swift international jetliner. Joseph Conrad, who stopped in Bangkok as a young sailor in 1888, described the city in amazement: "Great piles of masonry, King's Palace, temples, gorgeous and dilapidated, crumbling under the vertical sunlight, tremendous, overpowering, almost palpable." At a later time Somerset Maugham viewed the same "great piles of masonry" and told of "the surprise, the stupefaction almost, which assailed me when I saw these incredible buildings." Describing Bangkok's temples in *The Gentleman in the Parlor*, Maugham wrote: "They are unlike anything in the world, so that you are taken aback, and you cannot fit them into the scheme of the things you know. It makes you laugh with delight to think that anything so fantastic could exist on this sombre earth."

The Thai capital is still giving delight to Westerners. John Steinbeck, touring the Far East for *Newsday* in 1967, reported from Bangkok: "Right now we are wallowing in creature comforts, in music and laughter, in the beauty of women, the excitement of silk and gold and craftsmanship in wood and metal, in the sun sinking across the river and putting a red-gold glory in our rooms. We love it."

Perhaps Bangkok will never lose its exotic, story-book appeal. The venerable Oriental Hotel, on whose riverside terrace Maugham used to sip tall drinks and plot tales of intrigue while barges and sampans sailed close by, still dominates the waterfront. The temples are there, as fanciful and other-worldly as always. But parts of Bangkok have been catapulted suddenly into the late 20th Century. There are air-conditioned hotels, air-conditioned theatres, air-conditioned offices, and air-conditioned, neon-lit night clubs. Thai girls in "mod" clothes and Thai young men in the male equivalent of "groovy" apparel throng to discothèques, avant-garde art galleries, pizza palaces and hamburger joints. Jaguars, Mercedes-Benzes, and light, Japanese-style motorcycles are the preferred vehicles of the "in" generation in Thailand today, a country that looks eagerly to tomorrow.

New ways are considerably slower to arrive upcountry. But a traveler is very likely to hear rock 'n' roll music blaring from transistor radios in palm-thatched farm houses, and to see small-town girls astride Hondas zip past the wooden buses of yesteryear on country roads. This is a nation in the throes of great change, affected by Western influences with results that are not altogether calculable. But the influences appear to be on the whole beneficent, and to be leading to a richer and better life for most of the Thai people.

Thailand has allied itself firmly with the United States in opposing Communist aggression in Southeast Asia. It has taken the lead in efforts to effect a regional grouping of nations in this part of the world for long-range social and economic advance. A crossroads of people and of ideas, it is a major meeting place between East and West, a point of fusion between the old and the new. In many ways a pivotal nation in the Orient, Thailand is well worth the attention of thoughtful Westerners.

CHAPTER 1

The Land and the People

THAILAND was once an ocean bottom. Then, more than 300 million years·ago, most of the land that now comprises the peninsula of Southeast Asia rose slowly out of the sea to become part of a colossal continent that included today's Eurasia and Africa as well. For the next 200 million years, during which fishes and amphibians first appeared in the sea and dinosaurs rose to dominate the earth, this huge continent changed its shape continuously. Some 140 million years ago, the earth's crust began a period of violent upheavals. Behemoth rock layers were bent and snapped, while volcanoes erupted. Mountains reared up in many places, including much of the area of present-day Thailand. For eons following, wind and rain worked on the mountains of Southeast Asia, slowly but relentlessly grinding them down, until the whole area became a vast, featureless plain, its surface interrupted here and there by broad, shallow and very sluggish rivers.

Some 25 million years ago, the earth's crust again began to churn and heave, giving birth to spectacular mountain ranges. In Europe the Alps rose in sharp relief. In Asia the Himalayas thrust skyward, a titanic monument in granite. The rising Himalayas connected the land mass of India, then an island, to continental Asia, and extended in great ridges out across today's China and far to the southward. Mountains rippled through Yunnan and Burma to form the northern highlands of Thailand and the long ranges of the Malay Peninsula. A gigantic slab of sandstone was lifted into the air to become the Korat Plateau of northeastern Thailand. Here and there volcanoes spit out black basalt lava in which intense heat and underground pressure had fused mineral impurities into tiny pieces of brilliant stones: clear zircons, yellow topaz, deepred rubies and radiant blue sapphires — the famous Siamese gems.

Between 10,000 and 20,000 years ago, the melting of polar ice caps caused the world's oceans to rise, inundating vast areas of coastal lowlands. The southernmost part of Asia became what is known as the Sunda Shelf, the shallow bottom lying beneath the South China, Java, Celebes and Sulu Seas, as well as the Gulf of Thailand. Left above water were the myriad islands of Indonesia and the Philippines. Between the Asian mainland and Sumatra, the ridges of several mountain ranges escaped immersion to form the Malay Peninsula. Down the steep slopes of this spiny peninsula for millenia vigorous streams have been flowing, depositing in the valleys immense layers of sediment containing rich tin and tungsten ores.

Today Thailand is a tropical land of mountains, plateaus and alluvial plains, with an area of about 200,000 square miles — roughly the size of France. On the map, the country in outline looks something like the head of an elephant, trunk down, butting against Burma to the westward. The life rhythm of its plants, animals and people responds to the ebb and flow of the seasonal wind, or monsoon, a word derived from the Arabic term *mausim,* which means "season." In summer the air over Central Asia is heated by the sun and therefore expands, becomes lighter and rises skyward. Moist air over the oceans rushes toward the interior to take its place. In winter the Asian continent turns cold, and cool, dry air above it descends earthward and flows out toward the oceans. Thus each year in late May the moist southwest monsoon from the Indian Ocean starts to sweep inland, disgorging torrential rains over Thailand and its neighboring countries. By November the cool northeast monsoon arrives from continental China. As a result, most of Thailand has three distinct seasons: a humid, hot, rainy season from May to October; a cool, pleasant "winter" from November to February; and a dry and very hot transitional season of brilliant sunshine from March until May. Additional rain is brought by occasional tropical depressions and spent typhoons straggling in from the South China Sea. And from time to time during the dry season, towering black clouds explode in spectacular thunderstorms which are the coveted "mango showers."

Nature has been lavish in conferring on Thailand warm sunshine, copious rain and gentle winds for some 50 million years — even through the Ice Ages. Because of this, the land and waters of Thailand teem with an endless proliferation of plant and animal life. Even though crops have replaced jungle in many areas as a consequence of human habitation, more than half the country is still covered with forest today. The shallow seas adjacent to Thailand, continuously fed with sweet water and mineral-rich nutrients, heated to a year-round temperature of 70 degrees F., and having no strong currents or deep swells, abound with plankton, the tiny sea organisms which serve as the basic food of fishes. As a result, vast numbers of fish are to be found along the country's 1,600 miles of coast.

Thailand has four major geographical regions: the Continental Highlands, or Northern Thailand; the Central Plain, or Central Thailand; the Korat Plateau, or the Northeast; and Peninsular, or Southern Thailand. The Continental Highlands are a southern extension of the great plateaus of Tibet and Yunnan in China. Through these highlands, lofty, forest-covered ranges run north and south in parallel ridges, their peaks rising a mile and more into the sky. The 8,452-foot Doi Inthanon, Thailand's highest mountain, is in the extreme north. During the wet season, rain water continually drenches these mountains and runs down their steep sides in thousands of streams to collect into four big, southward-flowing rivers — tributaries of the mighty Menam Chao Phraya ("Mother of Noble Waters"), which empties into the Gulf of Thailand. Farther south, precipitous canyons give way to broad, high-lying valleys, where wood-burning trains chug past railway depots piled with stacks of cordwood to feed the fireboxes of the locomotives.

This is teak country. The tall, straight tree, with its large, oval leaves and candelabra of white blossoms in July and August, produces a beautifully grained, iron-like wood that has become a major Thai export. From the Northern valleys, huge teak logs begin their journey to the outside world at a leisurely pace, being floated downstream to Bangkok on a voyage that takes two years or more. In the teak forest the logs are moved about by trained elephants, which have never been outmoded as jungle derricks and bulldozers by 20th Century machinery.

Elephants do not have strong constitutions to match their muscle, and they cannot tolerate excessive heat. Teak

17

elephants must be given a four-month vacation each year, during which they get complete rest in some remote evergreen forest. On the job, the elephants usually work a five-hour day. In the evening after work, the mahouts tie their forefeet together and turn them loose to feed themselves in the jungle. The number of wild elephants in Thailand has steadily diminished in recent years, but the great beasts are still to be found in their natural habitat in several parts of the country.

Tigers and leopards prowl the forests of the Northern highlands, occasionally venturing out into clearings to prey on calfs and other farm animals. A Thai villager entering one of the denser jungle regions of this area will often take along a light-colored dog as a kind of lightning arrester; if a tiger or leopard should be encountered, the dog would be attacked first. Tigers here — as in other places — do not normally prey on humans, but sometimes become man-killers when weakened by old age and no longer able to hunt easily for such game as deer and wild mountain pigs. More feared than the tiger in Thailand is the big Himalayan bear, an aggressive carnivore that ranges the Northern mountains.

Where the Northern valleys have been cleared for planting, the principal crop is rice. The Northerners also plant garlic and red peppers, favorite Thai condiments, and they have extensive orchards of sweet, fragrant *litchi* and a related fruit called *lamyai* or *longan*. During the *lamyai* harvest each summer, young people of both sexes work as casual laborers in the orchards, and this leads to many weddings in the fall. When next year's *lamyai* are ready for harvest, so is a new crop of *lamyai* babies, most of whom are born in June.

South of the highlands is the Central Plain, the heartland of historic Siam and of the modern nation as well. Ringed by a horseshoe of mountains, this area used to be part of the Gulf of Thailand. Through countless centuries the highland rivers have carried silt into the gulf, creating new land. As the silting continues, the gulf shore keeps inching southward at a rate of about 15 feet a year. Bangkok, the leading port of Thailand, was once right on the gulf, but is now 20 miles inland. Near the city of Nakorn Sawan, where the upland rivers join to become the Chao Phraya, begins the lower part of the Central Plain which is called Bangkok Plain. This is a very fertile flatland whose slope toward the sea is so gentle that gulf tides reach the *klongs,* or canals, 60 miles in from the coast. Its original cover of rain forest has been completely displaced by cultivated crops.

Rice is the staple food of Thailand and the country's leading export. Two thirds of all Thai farmland — an area equal to two Netherlands — is given over to rice fields. On the coastal plains of the Peninsula, in the broad valleys of the North, on small patches of land in the arid Northeast, wherever water and soil permit, the Thai farmer plants rice. But the best rice country is the Central Plain.

Here, during the hot dry season, rivers and canals grow thin and fields are parched brown. The unrelenting sun produces a shimmering heat over all the land, and living things become listless and drowsy. Villagers spend long hours dozing under their thatched roofs. Dogs pant. Water buffaloes submerge their thick hides in mud holes. Banana and palm leaves droop and wilt in the 100-degree tropical air. But here and there the brown monotony of landscape is broken by the brilliant colors of flowering trees, shrubs and vines. Growing wild along river banks and in gardens as well are ten-foot poinsettias, straining their scarlet faces toward the sun. Cassia trees drape long racemes of yellow flowers in a golden cloudburst, or a shower of pastel pink, like a bridesmaid's gossamer gown. Every now and then one encounters the Flame of the Forest — an entire tree that appears to be on fire. Creepers, bougainvilleas and hibiscus cover trellises, fences and small trees with a wild profusion of colors: yellow, white, pink, cerise, brick red, lilac and pale blue. And everywhere is the heady, sensual fragrance of jasmine. This lovely white blossom, with its small, waxy petals, is the favorite flower of the Thai people. It is made into garlands to please the *phis,* or spirits, in roadside shrines, to bring luck to wild-riding taxi drivers, or to add a touch of perfume to the hair of lissome temple dancers.

The entire sleepy, sun-drugged delta plain bursts into life when the monsoon rains arrive. After the first downpours, farmers hitch up their water buffaloes to plow the newly-dampened fields for rice seeding. For five or six weeks the rice grows, while the rains increase, and then the seedlings must be transplanted. At transplanting time the fields are taken over by barefoot country women, sarongs tucked above their knees and palm-leaf hats like lampshades on every head. They slosh along in rows, pushing the rice plants into the soft mud. More rains come, and slowly the landscape turns into a checkerboard of delightful greens. One sees the movement of small, scurrying animals, and water birds such as storks, ibises and egrets. Swarms of insects appear. Now, as the rice grows, the water buffaloes can idly soak themselves in the canals, each animal usually carrying unnoticed on its broad back a gleeful naked boy, while several starlings peck busily for ticks around its ears and neck.

Rice needs a total of 70 inches of water to ripen, and on the Central Plain the yearly rainfall is only 40 to 60 inches. Nature supplies the additional water required each fall, when rivers swollen by upcountry runoff overflow their banks to flood the farmlands. The entire Central Plain becomes an inland sea, with islands of houses on stilts standing amid clusters of palms and bamboos. In some areas the flooding is so extreme, and lasts so long, that peasants must harvest their rice from boats, while fish ripple the water around them. The annual flood brings an accumulation of silt, which is left behind when the water recedes, to become a fresh layer of fertile soil for the rice fields.

Only half a century ago, many large species of wild animals roamed over parts of the Central Plain. Today they have all been pushed back to the jungle. But there is a tribe of noisy monkeys living in the sanctuary of a monkey shrine in Lopburi. The monkeys scramble out daily to forage for bananas and such — and often make away with hats and cameras lifted from unwary visitors. Among smaller creatures still to be found in the region are more than 30 varieties of bats, ranging from the big flying fox that used to glide over Bangkok at dusk, to a thimble-sized, insect-eating bat that can slip through window cracks. Coexisting peacefully with people in every home are the ubiquitous household lizards of tropical Asia. The five-inch gecko, so translucent and motionless on ceiling or wall that it resembles carved white jade, feeds on mosquitoes and other insect pests. The foot-long barking lizard is believed to bring good luck to the house in which it dwells. This reptile makes a gruff sound like a human basso, and sometimes startles people in the night by knocking its heavy tail against a door or window like a sudden visitor rapping.

East of Central Thailand is the Korat Plateau, a slightly tilted tableland that comprises one third of the country's area. This Northeast section is an infertile region of scrubby savanna, with a scattering of low hills and patches of scrawny jungle. During the rainy season it is a collection of transient lakes and swamps; when the monsoon shifts it becomes a dustbowl of swirling laterite, a fine red soil containing iron oxide, or rust. At some spots the iron content is so high that no grass or other plant will grow. These patches of dark ground are called *talat phi,* or "marketplace of the ghosts."

On the Korat Plateau, scaly anteaters forage among 10-foot-tall nests built by vast armies of termites. The farmers of this region grow rice, tobacco and *pokaeo*, or kenaf, a jute-like plant producing fibres which are used for making gunny sacks. Fortunately the Northeast is good country for raising cattle, since farm animals are of great importance to the Thai economy. The slow-moving, even-tempered, immensely powerful water buffalo is the Asian's waterproof tractor, unbeatable for getting through the sticky ooze of the rice fields. The bullock is used for plowing on drier farms, and is hitched in pairs to pull heavy carts in upland areas. From the Northeast come most of Thailand's 7,000,000 water buffaloes and 5,500,000 oxen — and many of its 12,000 tame elephants.

Peninsular Thailand is that region of the country which extends 500 miles south of Bangkok to form part of the Malay Peninsula. This crooked arm of land is only 15 miles wide at its narrowest point, the Isthmus of Kra, often envisioned as the site of a canal that would cut nearly a thousand miles from the shipping routes between ports on the Gulf of Thailand and the Indian Ocean. Flanked on two sides by tropical waters, the Peninsula catches rain against its high mountains from both the southwest and northeast monsoons. Unlike the rest of Thailand, it has two rainy seasons and one not-so-dry "dry" season — all hot — and it receives rainfall that in most places amounts to 80 inches or more annually. As a result, almost the entire area is covered with rain forests, edged along the coasts with mangrove swamps.

Warm tidal waters wash into these swamps and then retreat, to expose a bizarre landscape: from a sea of putrid muck rises a waist-high tangle of grotesque roots of the *pangkabai* mangrove, which has leather-like leaves and strange breathing organs that stick out of the mud like stalagmites. Up the estuaries of innumerable streams, amid dark green, stemless *chak,* or Nipa palms, pig-tailed monkeys swim in the shallows in search of crabs, and craggy crocodiles doze in the sun. For protection against crocodiles, the inhabitants of this region build parallel bamboo fences across streams at fording points, or else set off strings of firecrackers before stepping into the water. A large proportion of Thailand's crocodiles end up as wallets and handbags in Bangkok gift shops.

Inland a short distance is the magnificent spectacle of the tropical rain forest. Arboreal giants like *yang* and *tak-hien,* both valuable timber and resin trees, zoom straight upward as high as 175 feet, their thick crowns of green so close together at the top that only an occasional shaft of sunlight ever breaks through the foliage to strike the musty, leaf-cushioned forest floor. Some areas are taken over by clumps of bamboo, ranging from stubby dwarf varieties to 75-foot giants; elsewhere are huge ferns and sword-leafed screw pines. In the primeval rain forest of Thailand, more than 100 different kinds of trees can sometimes be counted in a single acre. In this shadowy green world, climbing vines and rattans entwine and endlessly embrace huge tree-trunks, sending down sprays of lacy air-roots from on high. Iridescent kingfishers flit across forest streams, while parakeets, pheasants and blue-tailed broad-bills murmur and screech and strut. Here tigers and night-prowling black panthers prey on tapirs and barking deer. Gibbons swing among lofty branches, and langurs high-dive from treetop to lesser treetop, feeding on leaves and fruits. Flying squirrels and flying lizards can be seen gliding through the forest canopy in slow, graceful arcs, while down below butterflies hover over fallen trees that are covered with thick moss, funguses and orchids. Thailand has 500 species of butterflies and 750 varieties of orchids.

Sultry, fecund and beautiful, the rain forest also can be dangerous to man. Besides tigers and black panthers, it has 56 species of snakes, 13 of them poisonous — including the cobra, king cobra and banded krait. Less deadly but nevertheless unpleasant to deal with are jungle leeches that attach themselves to humans and animals alike, sucking blood until they are as thick as a man's finger. Because the leeches secrete an anticoagulant that delays blood clotting, they leave wounds that are hard to heal.

Four-fifths of Thailand's 34 million people gain their living through agriculture, forestry, hunting or fishing. By far the largest number are engaged in farming. In addition to rice, the Thais grow a sizeable amount of corn — mainly for export as fodder — and in the Northeast kenaf has become a major cash crop. Along the east coast of the Peninsula the farmers plant cassava, a shrub of South American origin from whose starchy root comes tapioca. Other crops of some importance are cotton, tobacco, beans, sugar cane, peanuts, sesame, jute, ramie and various kinds of vegetables. Many Thais live off the forest as fruit pickers, while others cultivate orchards of their own. In the tropical jungles and on the farms grow tall durian trees whose huge fruit, looking like a green football with spikes, contains sweet but malodorous innards traditionally relished by the Thais. Thailand has a bewildering assortment of other tropical fruits, a list of which might begin with tangerine, orange, lime, custard apple, mango, papaya, breadfruit, jackfruit, mangosteen, rambutan, sapodilla, *litchi, lamyai* and 28 varieties of banana. Rubber trees are cultivated in the south, and coconut, areca and sugar palms in the central lowlands. Most of the country's coconut palms are on the Peninsula, where trained monkeys do the picking. For generations these obliging animals have been taught to climb the trees and throw down only ripened coconuts.

The areca palm, with its tall, straight trunk and fan-shaped top, is seen everywhere near villages. From earliest

24

days the Siamese have been chewing the nut of this palm in combination with the leaf of the betel pepper and lime, a mixture called "betel nut" that gives the individual a mild kick, and results over a period of time in scarlet lips and jet-black teeth. In old Siam these marks of the national habit were so fashionable that elderly ladies of the court who had lost their teeth used to sport false black dentures. Today Thai youths have stopped chewing betel nut. They are starting to chew gum.

The main source of protein in the national diet of Thailand is fish. An endless variety of species can be caught in the seas, rivers, canals, lakes, marshes, and even the flooded rice fields of the country. They are prepared fresh, dried, salted, pickled, smoked and fermented. Commercial fishermen go after schools of mackerel, herring and anchovies in the Gulf of Thailand. From the tiny, translucent *pla katak* anchovy comes the celebrated Siamese fish sauce, used in many of the national dishes. Other salt water fish harvested are mullet, pomfret, sole, the big *pla kapong* bass and the much-sought-after tropical shark. (Shark fins, which are relished by Chinese gourmets the world over, fetch enormous prices in the Far East.) Along rivers and canals, every household is equipped with a fishing pole or net or trap to get the family's daily supply of fresh carp, long, dappled murruls, egg-shaped kissing gourami, and bewhiskered catfish of all sizes from three-inch minnows to the gigantic *pla buk* variety of the Mekong River, which grows as big as a water buffalo.

In Thailand the life processes of many fish are attuned to the monsoon. Some species migrate seasonally; others, like the murrul, have acquired the ability to live for long periods out of water in order to survive the dry season when rivers shrink and sometimes disappear. The climbing perch, a favorite food fish, not only can breathe atmospheric air, but can crawl with its fins across a thousand feet of rough ground in search of water. During the dry season it buries itself as if in hibernation in the mud of a river bed, from which Thai fishermen dig it up. Fishing, in this instance, is done with a spade.

Mining is an industry of some importance along the Peninsula coasts, where tin and tungsten ores are extracted. Many of the miners here are jolly-looking young men from the Northeast. With their colorful *pakaomas* wrapped around them like sarongs, and habitually wearing carefree smiles as they work, they appear to the visitor more like members of a Hawaiian bachelor *luau* party than miners on the job. Coal and iron have been found in various parts of Thailand, but present surveys do not promise extensive quantities of these resources. Lignite, the "brown coal" which is intermediate between peat and bituminous coal, is in good supply, and is proving of increasing value as a fuel for power generators.

The Chao Phraya Valley, or Central Plain, which is the great, green rice bowl of the Thai nation, is home for the bulk of its population. This is the site of Bangkok, the capital and only cosmopolitan city, where some two million people live. There are only 12 other cities in the whole country with populations above 30,000. More than 80 per cent of the Thai people live in tiny villages. Compared to other Asian countries, Thailand's over-all population density of 170 per square mile is very low; the Central Plain alone could easily support twice as many people as it now does. However, national population has been increasing in recent times at three per cent per year — a rate among the highest in the world — as a result of the decrease in infant mortality and increase in life expectancy brought about by public health programs and rising living standards.

Although the Thais have been continuously absorbing new racial and cultural elements throughout their history, they are today an amazingly homogeneous people who share a common way of life and a distinct national identity. Those who live in the North and Northeast speak regional dialects and are sometimes called Lao-Thais, or simply Lao. But they are ethnically Thais.

Among Thailand's citizenship of about 34 million, the biggest ethnic minority are the Chinese, who number more than three million. Nearly half the population of Bangkok is of Chinese origin, and Chinese businessmen are very much in evidence in all the main cities. At one time, because of their tendency to live apart, to speak their own language, and to observe ancestral traditions rather than adopt new customs, the Chinese minority in Thailand threatened to become a problem to the country. In Indonesia and elsewhere in Southeast Asia, violence has erupted against alien Chinese residents whose loyalty came into question in times of nationalist fervor. But the Thai Government, starting in the 1940s, worked out a deliberate policy of absorbing the Chinese into the national population. Laws were enacted restricting Chinese language instruction in the schools and Chinese radio broadcasts, and limiting the further immigration of Chinese; at the same time, special tax advantages and economic opportunities were created for those who chose to become Thai citizens. The result has been a peaceful assimilation of all but a small fraction of the aliens. Today Chinese-Thais characteristically use Thai names, speak Thai, take Thai spouses, and call themselves Thai.

More difficult to assimilate, because of their Muslim religion, is the country's second largest minority, the 700,000 Thais of Malay origin. Living mostly in Thailand's four southernmost provinces adjacent to Malaya, they speak Malay, avoid eating pork, and in other ways follow the precepts of Islam. In the public schools of these provinces, where Muslims constitute four-fifths of the population, the Thai government has instituted courses in the

Malay language and the teachings of Mohammed.

Smaller minorities are comprised of some 300,000 descendants of ancient Cambodians, and 60,000 Mons, descended from Burmese war prisoners and refugees. There are about 60,000 Indians, mainly engaged in textile, jewelry and money-lending trades in the cities. The Thai population includes 140,000 indigenous Sui people in the Northeast, who are completely assimilated. The same cannot be said of the 30-odd hill tribes, a total of some 270,000 people who live principally in the mountains of northern and western Thailand. Most of these people are of Tibetan-Chinese stock, and drifted down from Southwest China and Burma during the last two centuries. Among the more important tribes are the Karen, Meo, Yao, Musso, Lahu, Ko and Lissaw. They wear distinctive tribal costumes and live a nomadic existence, practicing slash-and-burn agriculture and moving from mountain-top to mountain-top every two or three years. As a cash crop they have long raised poppies for making opium. Now the cultivation of poppies has been banned by the Thai government, and state agricultural experts have tried to introduce new crops to the hill tribes, as well as new methods of conserving their farmlands. But since these people remain in very remote areas — some tribes never settling below 5,000 feet — they are almost completely independent, and have largely maintained their traditional ways.

In the rain forests of the South dwell a curious tribe of several hundred Semangs, the remnant of an ancient race of pygmy Negritos who are believed to have been the original inhabitants of Thailand. The Semangs live in flimsy shelters made of leaves and twigs, wear very little clothing, and hunt with blow-pipe darts dipped in the poison of the upas tree. How these Stone-Age people were replaced by later arrivals in the land now called Thailand is part of another story.

CHAPTER 2

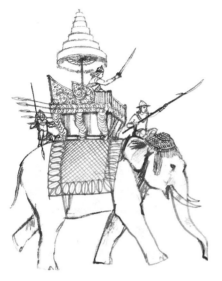

Years of Turmoil and Splendor

SOUTHEAST Asia, a rich and fertile region, easily accessible to man, has been the scene of migrations and counter-migrations, rivalry and warfare, empires built and empires destroyed, since the dawn of human history. Little is known about the very earliest inhabitants of the region. But in the late Stone Age continental Southeast Asia, including the area of present-day Thailand, was the home of pygmy Negritos and other primitive forest hunters, who were overrun and driven out of the best living spaces by Malay-type peoples in prehistoric times. Remnants of the Negritos are to be found today in remote mountain areas of the Malay Peninsula, Indonesia and the Philippines.

The newcomers evolved agricultural societies, domesticating the water buffalo and establishing rice culture as the basis of life in Southeast Asia — which it has remained to this day. In centuries of development, village settlements sometimes became towns, then city-states, and then kingdoms. At the time westernmost Europe was being Christianized, a great Indonesian empire was formed by the kings of Srivijaya, in Sumatra, who extended their dominion beyond the islands of the Malay Archipelago and up the Malay Peninsula to present-day southern Thailand.

A civilized people called Mons controlled a neighboring empire in continental Southeast Asia, with its capital city in Dvaravati, in what is now west-central Thailand. Both the kingdoms of Dvaravati and Srivijaya were greatly influenced by peaceful traders and missionaries from India, who brought Hindu culture and religion — Brahmanism and then Buddhism — into the whole geographical area.

In time the Mons gave way to conquest by the Khmers of Cambodia, another Indianized people whose empire, based on the city of Angkor, reached its zenith between 1000 and 1200 A.D. The Khmer civilization was notable for its religious cult identifying the king with the Hindu god, Siva, and temples of unprecedented magnificence erected in honor of the God-King. The renowned Angkor Wat is but one of numerous shrines of this character; the remains of another have been unearthed at Pimai, in northeastern Thailand.

The Khmers were succeeded in the area of the Chao Phraya River Valley by the Thais, a people whose story begins thousands of years earlier and in another land.

From somewhere in the vast reaches of central Asia, about 2000 B.C., tribes who called themselves Thai (the word means ("free") migrated into eastern China to settle in the area below the Yangtze River. About the time of Christ, the Thais came under heavy pressure from the Chinese — who were themselves feeling the push of northern invaders — and were gradually forced to move south.

In the Seventh Century the Thais established the strong, independent kingdom of Nanchao, on the mile-high Yunnan Plateau of southwest China. But many groups of Thais kept moving southward, trekking along the steep mountain valleys to Southeast Asia.

At the height of its power, Nanchao held sway over numerous neighboring states and was able to fight off periodic incursions by the Chinese. Some picturesque details of life in this early Thai kingdom are found in Chinese chronicles, which relate that high officials of Nanchao wore tiger skins, while soldiers wore leather armor and helmets and carried shields made of rhinoceros hide. The kingdom was divided into a dozen provinces, governed by cabinet ministers, viceroys, chamberlains, judges, generals and granary-keepers, under a king who appeared in public beneath a parasol of kingfisher feathers and flanked by a pair of fans, a hair plume and a royal axe. The people worshipped natural spirits and their own ancestors. They wove cotton, reared silkworms, made wooden implements, mined gold, and were allotted land according to their station. The whole society was brutally torn apart in 1253 when Kublai Khan, Mongol emperor of China and a descendant of Genghis Khan, swept into Yunnan with his terrible armies, conquered Nanchao and devastated the kingdom.

Thai migrants began drifting into Khmer territory in the Chao Phraya Valley about the year 700, and continued a gradual infiltration for several centuries. At first the Thais lived in subjection to the Khmers, occupying outlying regions and accepting inferior status as a minority people. By the 11th Century, however, Thai *muangs,* or city-states, were being founded in the upper reaches of the valley, and not long afterward the steady trickle of new arrivals from the north began to threaten the Khmer hegemony. In 1238 two Thai chieftains overthrew their masters, seized the northern Khmer capital of Sukhothai, and declared independence. This was the beginning of the nation that was to become Thailand. For the next 500 years Thai princes would be engaged in seesaw battling with Cambodians and Burmese — and sometimes with one another — for control of the fertile Chao Phraya Valley and adjoining territories.

Only 15 years after the Thai seizure of Sukhothai came the destruction of Nanchao, and the result was a great wave of Thai migration into the new city-state. Most of the earlier Thai migrants to Southeast Asia had settled in northern Burma; these people were called Shans or Thai-Yai (Major Thai). The bulk of the refugees fleeing after the fall of Nanchao came to rest in the Chao Phraya Valley, the central region of present-day Thailand; settlers here became known as Siamese or Thai-Noi (Minor Thai). A later wave of Thai migrants found their home in the area of today's northern Thailand and Laos, and are called Thai-Lao or simply Lao.

The first Thai king of Sukhothai — it means "Dawn of Happiness" — was crowned Sri Intaratitya, but he is better known as Phra Ruang, a name associated with a heroic figure in an ancient Thai legend. Over the centuries, the life of this "founding father" has acquired an aura of myth. Among other unearthly accomplishments, it is said that Phra Ruang could carry water in baskets and turn fish bones back into live fish.

Outshining even Phra Ruang, however, was his third son, King Rama Kamheng — warrior, statesman, scholar, lover, devout Buddhist and discriminating patron of the arts. Beginning his four-decade reign around 1275, Rama Kamheng turned Sukhothai from a struggling city-state into a renowned kingdom, whose territory extended eastward to include the city of Luang Prabang in present-day Laos, and westward to the shores of the Andaman Sea. Opening direct diplomatic and cultural relations with

China, he visited Peking soon after Marco Polo had left that illustrious capital. On his second visit to Peking, in 1300, he brought back technical aid in the form of 500 Chinese potters, who set up kilns in Sukhothai and nearby Sawankaloke. For a century and a half, Sawankaloke pottery was eagerly sought after by traders from many countries. Today it is a prized collector's item.

The Sukhothai era was a happy one in Thai history. Among rolling, teak-forested hills, King Rama Kamheng governed a gentle people with fatherly affection from his mile-square capital, a city protected by strong walls and moats and made green by an earthen dam backing up a reservoir of some 33 million cubic feet of water to last through the dry season. Sukhothai had more than 80 Buddhist monasteries, whose ruins still evoke a sense of beauty and majesty. The greatest masterpieces of Thai sculpture are found among Sukhothai bronze Buddhas, which are human in form but ethereal in spirit. Rama Kamheng maintained close contacts with Ceylon, the great center of fundamentalist Buddhism, and many Ceylonese monks came to Sukhothai to fortify this doctrine among the Thai people.

But the great king is remembered most of all for his invention of the Thai script, which established an alphabet derived from Mon, Khmer and Sanskrit originals. On a huge stone, discovered centuries later, he had his ideology inscribed in the new written language: "This Muang Sukhothai is good. In the water there are fish; in the fields there is rice. . . . Whoever wants to trade in elephants so trades. Whoever wants to trade in horses so trades. Whoever wants to trade in silver and gold so trades." He ordered a tremendous bell hung from a palace gate, to be tolled by anyone who wished to summon the king personally to hear grievances and render justice. At festivals the people of Sukhothai brought offerings to the temples in the form of cowrie shells, areca nuts, flowers and colorful cushions — moving in gay processions, the men and women singing, playing musical instruments and dancing, as their descendants do today. The quintessence of Thai gaiety and love of life is to be found in another part of Rama Kamheng's famous inscription: "Whoever wants to play plays. Whoever wants to laugh laughs. Whoever wants to carol carols."

The splendor that was Sukhothai began to fade immediately after Rama Kamheng's death, and under his successors the kingdom's territory was sliced off bit by bit by covetous neighbors. Only 61 years after the great king died, Sukhothai became the vassal of Ayudhya, an emergent Thai city-state to the south. Another 60 years, and Sukhothai disappeared altogether.

When founded by King Rama Tibodi in 1350, Ayudhya was a modest settlement of teakwood houses, surrounded by a mud rampart topped with wooden spikes. But the kingdom was destined to see more than four centuries of imperial splendor, of pageantry and royal pomp, heroism and undying loyalty, as well as intrigue, treachery and bloody war. Growing quickly in power during the second half of the 14th Century, Ayudhya — which in time became known to the world as Siam — absorbed its neighboring Thai states, including Sukhothai, and began more than a century and a half of sporadic wars with Chiengmai, a powerful Thai kingdom in the north. The declining Khmers, although driven back to Cambodia, staged repeated invasions of Ayudhya, once kidnapping 7,000 Siamese to become their slaves. In prompt retaliation, the Ayudhyan army marched to the Cambodian capital of Angkor, captured that city, and returned with no fewer than 90,000 war prisoners — whose descendants now live in northeastern Thailand. This ended for a time the threat from Cambodia.

In 1448 began the 40-year reign of King Boroma Trailokanat, or Trailok, who centralized and tightened the administration of the Siamese kingdom. He systematized the *Sakdina,* the social code originating in the days of Nan-chao, which defined the status of citizens in accordance with land holdings. A milestone of King Trailok's regime was the Palace Law, setting forth detailed regulations for palace administration and court ceremonies, as well as punishment for various offenses against the crown. The penalty for rocking the king's barge or whispering at a royal audience was death; for seducing a palace lady, torture and then death. Frightful as these punishments seem today, it should be remembered that similar cruelties were practiced by the royalty of medieval Europe. (Furthermore, harsh sentences in old Siam were often commuted or offenders pardoned by the king — to conform to Buddhist principles of mercy and thus gain merit for the sovereign.) The Palace Law decreed proper respect for aristocratic criminals; erring princes and lords of high rank wore gold shackles, while lesser noblemen had to be content with silver shackles.

Not long after Vasco da Gama's historic voyage around the Cape of Good Hope, the Portuguese captured the important Muslim trading center of Malacca, on the Malay Peninsula. From here they sent an envoy, Duarte Fernandez, to Siam. He hitchhiked on a Chinese junk, reaching Ayudhya in 1511 to establish a treaty of friendship and commerce. This was Siam's first diplomatic contact with the West. Many other Portuguese followed Fernandez to Ayudhya to trade, to preach, and to serve as mercenaries in the Siamese army. The kings of Siam not only allowed the Portuguese visitors to spread the doctrine of Christianity among their subjects, but also permitted them to erect and maintain a huge wooden cross in a public place in Ayudhya. However, the Westerners were less successful in converting the Siamese to their religion than in imparting their knowledge of firearms and fortifications. Many

Portuguese married Siamese women, and faintly European features may still be detected among some of their descendants in Thailand today.

The mid-16th Century stands as an ill-starred era in Thai history. The court of Ayudhya was almost destroyed by plots and counter-plots to seize the royal power. A five-year-old king reigned for five months and was then murdered by a usurper, who made himself king — only to be poisoned by his wife. She put her 11-year-old son on the throne and made her paramour the regent. In a short time the regent had the boy-king done away with and seized the crown, but was himself slain by noblemen loyal to the previous usurper. These events, coming all within a span of 15 years, so demoralized the kingdom that an aggressive Burmese monarch was emboldened to invade Siam. Crossing the border with 300,000 men, 3,000 horses and 700 elephants, he laid siege to Ayudhya, unsuccessfully, for four months.

Fearing another invasion, the king of Ayudhya made massive defense preparations, and ordered the capture of 300 elephants to be trained for combat use. In the catch were seven white elephants, which are considered sacred in Southeast Asia; jubilantly the Siamese king proclaimed himself Lord of the White Elephants. Thereupon, a new Burmese king insolently demanded two white elephants for himself, and when he was turned down he declared war. An expedition against the Siamese netted him royal hostages, tribute, and no fewer than four white elephants. A few years later Burma again besieged Ayudhya. The city fell in 1569, and Siam remained a humiliated and exploited vassal state of Burma for the next 15 years — a period during which Cambodia renewed its incursions into Siamese territory.

But fortunes turned, and the Siamese kingdom revived.

Ayudhya was restored to sovereignty and power by the greatest warrior in Thai history, the fabulous Black Prince. Prince Naresuan, who got his nickname because of his swarthy complexion, was the son of the vassal king of Ayudhya under the Burmese. In 1584 Naresuan renounced his father's subservience to Burma, rallied an army, and started eight years of determined resistance, turning back five full-scale invasions by the Burmese. During this period his father died and Naresuan became king.

In 1592 a final invasion of Ayudhya was attempted by 250,000 Burmese under their crown prince, Min Chit Swa. In the confusion of a battle the elephants carrying King Naresuan and his brother dashed wildly into a sea of Burmese troops, becoming separated from the rest of the Ayudhyan army. The two Siamese warriors found themselves face to face with none other than the Burmese crown prince. Naresuan challenged him to a duel on elephantback. The elephants charged at each other, and Naresuan's leather helmet was cut through by the sword of Min Chit Swa. They dashed at each other a second time, and Naresuan's sword slashed into the shoulder of the Burmese prince, who fell dead from his elephant. After the king's personal triumph, his soldiers completely routed the invaders and eventually recovered a sizable strip of lost territory. To this day Thai youths are enthralled by the story of the heroic duel fought by their great national liberator on his elephant mount.

Having disposed of the Burmese threat, King Naresuan turned his attention to the east, where marauding bands of Cambodians were still causing trouble. He mounted a punitive expedition into Cambodia in 1593, and made that country a vassal state. Naresuan also took the offensive against Burma, launching several invasions to capture seaports on the Indian Ocean. During one of these campaigns, in 1605, the warrior king fell sick and died. He left Ayudhya with its territories enlarged and its enemies broken, secure in looking ahead to a long period of affluence and peace.

It was a stimulating era that came next, an era of cosmopolitan growth and increasing contact with the outside world. For sophistication and splendor, the court of Siam was rivalled in Asia only by that of Imperial China. The territory taken from the Burmese by Naresuan included the important port of Mergui, on the Bay of Bengal. Previously it had been necessary for 17th Century traders moving goods between the Indian Ocean and the China Sea to make a tedious voyage around the long finger of the Malay Peninsula; now it was possible to substitute an overland shortcut between Mergui on the west side of the peninsula and Ayudhya on the east. As a major transshipment point, Ayudhya thus became a thoroughfare for travelers between Europe and the Orient.

Siam's second treaty of commerce with a European power was made in 1598, when King Naresuan entered into an agreement with the Spaniards of Manila, many of whom came to reside in Ayudhya and do business there. They were followed in subsequent years by the Dutch, the English, the Danes and, in 1662, the French. The kings of Siam flung open their gates and put out the welcome mat — and at times the red carpet — for strange-mannered European envoys, traders, mercenaries, missionaries and soldiers of fortune. Soon the city of Ayudhya was overflowing its ramparts for miles around with warehouses, wharves and residential settlements for the Portuguese, Chinese, Malays, Dutch, English, Japanese and French who accepted the Siamese hospitality.

Unfortunately, this generous attitude toward foreigners was rudely repaid in 1664, during the reign of King Narai, when the Siamese had their first taste of gunboat diplomacy. The Dutch used armed threats to force a treaty on Siam, gaining for the Dutch East India Company a monopoly in hides and the first guarantee of extraterritorial rights to be extracted from the kingdom. Dutch citizens living in Siam were placed under the administration of their own national government, and were no longer subject to Siamese law.

Seeking to check the increasingly aggressive Hollanders, King Narai cast around for the possibility of forming an alliance with another European power. The first French Jesuits had just at that time arrived in Ayudhya, and among the missionaries there happened to be a man who was an expert architect and engineer. His technical knowledge was eagerly sought by Narai for the construction of Western-style fortifications to hold off any Dutch attack. Narai gave money and land for churches to the Jesuits, and they in turn helped him to forge friendly diplomatic links with King Louis XIV of France and Pope Alexander VII.

In 1675 an English ship named *Phoenix* dropped anchor at Ayudhya, and down its gangplank walked a 25-year-old Greek adventurer who was destined to play a remarkable role in the mercurial affairs of the Siamese kingdom. Constantine Phaulkon started his career by running away from home on the Ionian island of Cephalonia to go to sea as a cabin boy. By the time of his arrival in Ayudhya, he had become a factor, or trade agent, for a Captain George White, one of numerous English free-lancers in the wide-open trading arena of the Far East. Such persons were regarded with hostility as "interlopers" by the British East India Company, which controlled a large share of the overseas commerce of Asia and did everything in its power to discourage English traders from operating on their own. Nevertheless, both White and his protégé, Phaulkon, became influential members of Ayudhya's international set.

Five years after his arrival, Phaulkon was taken into

the Siamese government as assistant to the Lord of the Treasury. The young Greek won the attention of the king when he suggested an ingenious solution to the problem of weighing a massive cannon: by first putting the cannon aboard a barge and marking the waterline, then removing the cannon and loading the barge with bricks until the barge sank to the same level; the bricks could then be weighed easily in separate lots. Phaulkon rose swiftly in status and influence, becoming a *chao phraya,* or noble lord, of Siam, as well as the principal adviser and confidant of King Narai. At the height of his power he lived regally in two palaces, where people approached him on all fours, as they approached the king himself. He had a beautiful Japanese wife who was known, in a phonetic approximation of her name, as Dame Golden Horseshoe.

King Narai, sick with dropsy, turned over to Phaulkon more and more of the affairs of state. The young Greek strongly allied himself — and Siam — with the French, whose political influence grew to such an extent that serious resentment developed among the Siamese courtiers, many of whom were distressed to see their country seemingly overrun with Frenchmen and virtually ruled by a Greek. It was around this time that the word *farang* was coined, from "Français," a term used to this day in Thailand to denote any Westerner. When Narai became hopelessly ill, in 1688, the leader of the anti-French faction among the nobility, Phra Petraja, was made regent. His first act was to slay Narai's adopted son and heir-apparent. Next he arrested Phaulkon in his summer palace, imprisoned him and executed him for treason. Imprisoned also, but then released, was Dame Golden Horseshoe. Years later, in an astonishing sequel of events, she turned up as a superintendent of the Royal Kitchen.

When King Narai died, Petraja was made king amid rising popular feeling against France. He forced the French — and other Europeans as well — to leave the country; only a few missionaries were allowed to remain. Siam slammed shut its door to the West and for nearly a century and a half went its own way. During this entire period, the country's only diplomatic contact was with China.

About the middle of the 18th Century Burma renewed its invasions of Siamese territory, and in early 1766 Ayudhya was once again within Burmese gunsights. The siege lasted for 14 months, a terrible period during which hunger, disease and a great fire heaped suffering on top of suffering for the defenders. To give the impression that they had more male protectors than they really had — and to make it harder for Burmese soldiers to drag them off as captives — the women of Ayudhya cut off their long hair. The "Siamese bob" lasted as a national style until early in the 20th Century.

On April 7, 1767, Ayudhya fell — and all its fortifications and dwelling places, its teeming bazaars and sedate, teak-doored libraries, its opulent palaces and glittering temples were razed to the ground by the Burmese. The devastation was so thorough that even Buddha images were hacked to pieces, although the invaders were themselves Buddhists. The king of Ayudhya was slain. Other members of the royal household and hundreds of aristocrats and high officials were taken captive, as were tens of thousands of peasants and soldiers. Men, women and children were tortured to reveal their real or imagined hidden wealth. Cart after cart and elephant after elephant went westward toward Burma, loaded with plundered jewels, firearms, and fragments of gold Buddha images. Nearly all the books and written records of the entire Ayudhya era and before went up in smoke. Ayudhya the Glorious and Impregnable, a city of more than a million inhabitants, after 417 years, three dynasties and 33 kings, was no more.

A mighty kingdom had come to an abrupt, catastrophic

end — or so it seemed in that dark hour for Siam. But the Siamese phoenix would rise from the ashes of Ayudhya and shine forth again in even greater glory — and all because of a half-Chinese guerrilla leader named Phya Taksin. A general of the Siamese army who slipped out of the doomed Ayudhya with 500 soldiers just before it fell, Taksin established a foothold on the unoccupied eastern shore of the Gulf of Siam. There many patriotic Siamese joined him to fight the Burmese. Within half a year his army had grown ten-fold, and he easily captured the town of Thonburi, on the Chao Phraya River, to begin the liberation of Siam. Taksin proclaimed himself king, drove out the Burmese, and made Thonburi his capital. Ayudhya was beyond rebuilding. Siam had by this time disintegrated into five separate states, and King Taksin spent seven years in putting down opposition and unifying the country. During his 15-year reign he also turned back four massive new invasions from Burma, and restored Siamese suzerainty over Cambodia, Chiengmai, and the Laotian principalities of Luang Prabang and Vientiane.

Then King Taksin developed paranoic tendencies. He imagined that he had turned into the Buddha, suspected his supporters of disloyalty, and persecuted them out of his own delusions. A palace revolt brought down the mad king, who was imprisoned and subsequently executed. Today in the Temple of the Dawn in Thonburi, a gilded statue of King Taksin gazes down at the daily crush of tourists, most of whom take him for just another Buddha — an ironic turn of fate unexpectedly fulfilling in a way poor King Taksin's demented fancy.

By popular acclaim, Chao Phraya Chakri, a nobleman who had been an able general under Taksin, was elevated to the throne in April, 1782. Known as King Phra Buddha Yot Fa Chulalok, or King Rama I, his coronation marked the beginning of Thailand's currently reigning Chakri

Dynasty, and it took place in the same year the United States was recognized as a nation by Great Britain after the American Revolution. King Rama I moved the capital across the river to the village of Bangkok, re-naming it *Krungthep Phra Maha Nakorn Amon Ratanakosindra,* or Royal City of Angels, Jewel Abode of Indra. *Krungthep* is still the official and popularly preferred Thai name for the capital, but the city is internationally known by its original name, which means Village of Olive Trees. King Rama I patterned the new city after Ayudhya. He built the magnificent Grand Palace and the Temple of the Emerald Buddha as they stand today — displacing a Chinese settlement that was relocated in Sampeng, now Bangkok's Chinatown. And he began the long and difficult task of national reconstruction, which involved a revival of state ceremonies, codification of the laws that survived Ayudhya, organization of the Buddhist scriptures, and restoration of the traditional Siamese arts.

His successors, Rama II and III, continued the work of King Rama I in building and restoring great monasteries and in dispensing literary and religious patronage. The Temple of the Dawn, with its colossal, porcelain-studded towers and gigantic demons, and Wat Sutat, whose rooflines Somerset Maugham described as the most beautiful of all, were built during the reign of these kings. Rama II's most notable achievement, however, was his reopening of Siam to the West after 130 years of isolation. In 1818 he permitted a Portuguese consul to stay in Bangkok. The British returned to Siam four years later. American missionaries arrived for the first time in 1828, from China, and introduced into Siam both the printing press and the science of vaccination. Because they were equipped to give medical treatment, these early American missionaries were called *moh,* which is the word for physician. Today all American missionaries in Thailand are called *moh.*

The renewed dealings between Siam and the West were not without minor difficulties and frictions at the point of contact. First was the linguistic barrier. At the time, not a single Siamese could speak any European language, aside from a few Portuguese-Siamese descendants who knew a kind of pidgin Portuguese. The British envoy, therefore, had to speak in English to one interpreter, who translated his remarks into Malay, which was then translated into Siamese by a second interpreter. A more formidable barrier was cultural. Partly because of their ignorance of Asian custom, British envoy Sir James Brook and American envoy Joseph Ballestier both failed to get new treaties which they sought from Siam in 1850. The Siamese traditionally attached great importance to the seal of royalty, treating a king's document with the same respect as his person. They were insulted when Sir James called upon King Rama III without bearing any credentials from Queen Victoria; the ambassador had nothing but a paper signed two years before by the Governor General of India. Even more annoying was his supercilious attitude toward Asians, whom he clearly regarded as inferiors. Ballestier went to the Siamese court with an American missionary named Smith as interpreter, and the missionary carried in one hand an umbrella and in the other hand a box containing the "king's document" as if it were a pair of overshoes. Ballestier never got to see the Siamese ruler at all. Such diplomatic *faux pas* would be unthinkable today, but they were regrettably common to the early meetings of West with East.

In the latter half of the 19th Century and first decade of the 20th, Siam was governed by perhaps its most capable and farseeing kings: Rama IV, better known as King Mongkut, and his son, Rama V, or King Chulalongkorn. In six decades devoted to the encouragement of social reform and technical progress, these two rulers changed Siam from an insular, feudal kingdom into a modern nation, and enabled it to weather the tidal wave of European colonialism that engulfed all the neighboring countries of Southeast Asia.

When King Rama III died, his half-brother and successor, Prince Mongkut, had been a monk in a Buddhist monastery for 27 years. During this long priesthood, Prince Mongkut learned Pali, the ancient language of India in which the original Buddhist scriptures were written. He acted to purify Siamese Buddhism by founding the Dhammayutta sect within the monkhood, a scholarly group which takes its doctrine entirely from the Pali writings. A philosopher and theologian, Mongkut also had a lively curiosity about the world and a great respect for science. Stimulated by discussions with French and American missionary friends, he learned world geography, astronomy, Latin and English. Biographers say that he knew and understood Christianity quite as well as Buddhism.

Before succeeding to the throne, King Mongkut discovered in the overgrown ruins of Sukhothai and brought to Bangkok King Rama Kamheng's famous inscribed stone tablet celebrating the virtues of freedom and individual enterprise, and this provided great inspiration for his reign. He was also strongly influenced by the visible role of Europe and the United States in Far Eastern affairs. Mongkut was one of the first to sense the freshening West wind in 19th Century Asia, and he trimmed the sails of Siam accordingly. The event that most impelled his modernization of the country along Western lines was the Opium War of 1840, in which once-proud China suffered a humiliating defeat at the hands of the British. (Britain fought the war to maintain the Chinese opium trade — because the rulers of China had tried to stop this commerce, and British profits as international carriers of opium were threatened.) The prestige of the Celestial Empire was so legendary that most Siamese believed the face-saving claim of Chinese mandarins after the surrender that China had granted the British terms merely to avoid petty annoyance. Mongkut and a handful of others knew better: if Siam were to avoid China's fate, it must modernize.

At his coronation in 1851, King Mongkut broke some centuries-old precedents; he invited foreign residents to the ceremony, and he exempted them from the traditional requirement of prostrating themselves before the king. As monarch, he startled his subordinates by telling them to approach him with problems at any time instead of going through the usual bureaucratic channels. It had long been the custom for noblemen and officials of Siam to pledge loyalty to the king at an annual ceremony; King Mongkut shocked conservatives of the court by pledging *his* loyalty to the *people* on the same occasion. Ever since the days of Rama Kamheng, first a bell and then a drum had stood outside the royal palace, to be sounded by common citizens seeking justice from the king. Through the centuries the drum had become a silent relic. After his public invitation to use it had failed to bring forward his subjects, King Mongkut came out of the palace twice a week, on a regular schedule, to listen to anyone who wanted to speak to him about any grievance.

The wise king invited many foreign advisers to serve in his administration, and with their help he minted Siam's first modern currency and built a number of roads, including Bangkok's New Road — the first dry thoroughfare in a land of canals. Seeking rapprochement with the West, he welcomed Sir John Bowring when this British envoy came to Bangkok in 1855 to negotiate a new trade agreement. The two men became lifelong friends. A British treaty was followed by similar pacts with the United States, France and other European powers. The agreements hardened extraterritorial privileges for Westerners in Siam — a loss of sovereignty that would not be recovered by Siamese kings for three fourths of a century — and they ended a number of lucrative royal monopolies in trade revenues. But by increasing the volume of international trade, the treaties undoubtedly benefited the Siamese nation.

Mongkut's friendship with the West did not entirely immunize Siam from colonial encroachment in an era when European imperialism was at its height. In 1863 it became apparent that the French government intended to take possession of Cambodia, then a Siamese tributary. Knowing that armed resistance would be hopeless, King Mongkut persuaded the British — who had rival interests in Southeast Asia — to arrange a treaty by which Siam relinquished most of Cambodia to France but reaffirmed its sovereignty over two of the westernmost Cambodian provinces. His relationship with the United States was entirely cordial. In response to a gift of some 200 government publications from President Buchanan, King Mongkut wrote a letter to the American president offering him a supply of war elephants. By the time the letter arrived, the presidency was occupied by Abraham Lincoln, a man who might well have found use for such exotic battlefield equipment. But in view of technical problems, Mr. Lincoln graciously declined the king's military aid.

In 1868 King Mongkut died of a fever caught in the Peninsular jungle, where he had gone on a camping trip with Western friends to observe an eclipse of the sun — to the end a scholar and devotee of science. Among his last words was a farewell message in Pali to his former colleagues of the brotherhood of monks, asking them "not to give way to grief nor to any sudden surprise, since death must befall all creatures." King Mongkut is revered in memory throughout Thailand, and is regarded by Western historians as one of the most enlightened and progressive rulers of recent times. His reign was described by an American missionary who knew him well as "the mildest and best heathen government on the face of the globe." Ironically, the image of King Mongkut before the world is that created by a self-righteous Victorian school mistress and vulgarized by Hollywood as a sybaritic character in the popular musical, *The King and I*.

The school mistress was Mrs. Anna Leonowens, a British widow whom King Mongkut employed in 1862 to give English lessons to some of the 82 sons and daughters he had by his 35 wives. A word might well be said here about polygamy, which was practiced in 19th Century Siam, and is still found in a number of Asian countries. In old Siam it was not only a man's prerogative but a king's duty to have many wives. Multiple royal marriages were insurance that there would be plenty of heirs to the throne. The marriages provided links of family loyalty to the king's top aides, and were important as instruments of diplomacy — drawing nations to one another by blood ties instead of today's more tenuous ties of foreign aid. King Mongkut was constantly besieged by noblemen wishing to offer their daughters to him in marriage, causing the king eventually to declare that he had more wives than he wanted. In fact, he devised an ingenious law enabling his wives to "resign" and marry commoners if they so desired.

When Anna Leonowens returned to England after five years in Bangkok, she wrote a book entitled *A British Governess at the Court of Siam*, which made it appear that morality in the Siamese kingdom began with the arrival of pious Anna. The book sold so well that she wrote a second one, *The Romance of the Harem* (now reissued as *Siamese Harem Life*), which is described by present-day Western scholars as an absurdly lurid story drawing together a collection of worn clichés about Oriental harems from Peking to Constantinople. A. B. Griswold, an American authority on Thailand and recent biographer of King Mongkut, has cited numerous examples of plagiarism and fictionalization in the work of Mrs. Leonowens. But her two books became the basis of Margaret Landon's best-seller, *Anna and the King of Siam,* and this in turn inspired the highly successful Broadway musical and world-famous film, *The King and I.* In an age when the image often counts more than the substance, millions of people look unknowingly at Thailand through the eyes of Anna Leonowens.

King Mongkut's son and successor, Chulalongkorn, was 16 when his father died. Before coming of age to ascend the throne at 21, the young prince traveled extensively in Malaya, Java and India, learning about his neighbors — and getting a good look at Western colonialism in the process. What he saw convinced him that Siam must keep itself free from control by any of the European powers.

At the coronation of King Chulalongkorn in 1873, Siamese subjects present at the ceremony all prostrated themselves as tradition dictated when in the presence of royalty. The moment he was crowned, Chulalongkorn announced that henceforth there would be no prostration before the king. In one of the most dramatic moments in Siamese history, the entire court rose to its feet at the new king's words. It was the keynote of Chulalongkorn's forward-looking rule. In his 42-year reign he extended education in Siam, developed roads and railroads, reformed the civil administration, initiated postal and telegraph services, and sent many promising young people to study in Europe — students who would later return to serve in the Siamese government. He also abolished slavery, only three years after abolition was completed in the United States.

Chulalongkorn's Siam faced continuing threats from the spread of British and French colonialism. In the late 1880's it had to yield to France several large pieces of territory that became present-day Laos. In 1896 France and Britain agreed to make Siam a buffer state between their holdings in Southeast Asia. Siam was recognized as a sovereign kingdom, and treaties were signed limiting extra-territorial privileges for French and British citizens. Nevertheless, during the next 13 years France sliced off more Siamese territory, incorporating four eastern provinces into the French colony of Cambodia — an historic fact that goes a long way toward explaining the continuing disputes between Thailand and Cambodia in the present era. The British took four provinces in the south and merged them into Malaya. Outlying regions of the country were lost to the European empire-builders. But through skillful diplomacy King Mongkut and King Chulalongkorn succeeded in preserving the main body of Siam as an independent nation.

Two of Chulalongkorn's sons succeeded him as the next kings of the Chakri Dynasty. King Vajiravudh, or Rama VI (1910-1925), was the first Siamese ruler to be educated abroad. He studied in England, and held the rank of general in the British army. An intellectual as well as a soldier, he wrote plays and essays, translated Shakespeare into Siamese, and is credited with introducing compulsory education into the kingdom. Siam joined the Allies of World War I in 1917, and sent an expeditionary force to Europe. It was prompt in becoming a member of the League of Nations in 1919. During the Paris Peace Conference, Siam urged upon the United States and the European powers its desire for judicial independence, and thereafter extraterritorial rights for Westerners were gradually eliminated.

King Prajadhipok, or Rama VII (1925-1935), also educated in England, was the last monarch to hold absolute power in Siam. On June 24, 1932, a group of young government and military leaders who had been influenced by Western political ideas sent a demand to the king for the establishment of a constitutional monarchy. The king, who had himself concluded that Siam was ready for constitutionalism, promptly acceded to the revolutionists' demand. Three years later he abdicated. The throne that he vacated passed to his nephew, King Ananda Mahidol, or Rama VIII. Upon Ananda's death in 1946, his Swiss-educated brother, Bhumibol Adulyadej, became King Rama IX.

During World War II Japanese troops landed in Siam — by now called Thailand — and the government was forced to declare war on the Allies. This declaration, exacted under duress, was never accepted as genuine by the United States, and a Free Thailand movement was gaining momentum both within the country and overseas when the Japanese defeat came. In 1946 Thailand joined the United Nations. Since then Bangkok has been chosen as the permanent location for the United Nations Economic Commission for Asia and the Far East (ECAFE), and the regional site of several other U.N. agencies. In response to the 1950 U.N. resolution on Korea, Thailand was the first Asian nation to send troops to Seoul. Today Bangkok is the headquarters of SEATO, the Southeast Asia Treaty Organization, a defense alliance involving Australia, New Zealand, Pakistan, the Philippines, Thailand, France, Britain and the United States.

Thailand's foreign policy since World War II has been consistently friendly to the West and wary toward Communist aggression in Asia. Living within the shadow of Red China, with Vietnam almost next door and an ever-present threat of Communist infiltration at home, the Thais are today cooperating closely with their allies to maintain the independence of all Southeast Asian nations. It is not by accident that these people have always called their country *Muang Thai,* or the Land of the Free.

CHAPTER 3

Where the Spirit Reigns

IT IS full moon in May, or Visakha Bucha, the date that commemorates the Buddha's birth, Enlightenment and death. In the temple hall of the great Bangkok monastery, Wat Sutat, the 30-foot Phra Srisakayamuni Buddha, surrounded by classical murals and exquisitely carved teak doors, gazes down in benign majesty from beneath a nine-tiered parasol at the 50 chanting monks and 1,000 worshippers below. The latter are crouching, kneeling, or moving about on the marble floor, to pray and to offer flowers, candles and incense sticks. Outside, some 3,000 additional worshippers are waiting in the monastery courtyard for the ceremonial circumambulation, a clockwise procession three times around the temple structure.

Now the abbot and his monks start the procession on

the terrace. Men, women and children in festive mood, each with a lighted candle, some also carrying white lotus blossoms, begin to parade around the perimeter of the spacious courtyard — an area enclosed by galleries containing 160 gilded Buddha images and dotted with greystone Chinese pagodas and bronze horses. The 4,000 slow-moving, flickering candles and the full moon above create a deeply impressive shadow-play of otherworldliness in the night. But there is no solemnity here, no ceremonial stiffness on the part of the participants, nothing but good-natured jostling and unaffected smiles. A woman loses a shoe. She shrugs her shoulders, takes off the other shoe, and laughingly continues her walk.

The guttural sound made by Brahman priests blowing on conch shells marks the auspicious moment fixed by the stars at Pramane Ground, Bangkok's public square, as the King and Queen and 100,000 others watch. In an embroidered white robe and a pagoda-shaped white hat, the Lord of the Harvest steps to an altar made of banana and sugarcane stalks, and there, shrouded in incense smoke, he offers a pig's head to the Hindu deities whose favors are being invoked. The Lord of the Harvest is a government official of high rank who has been chosen for his role in the yearly ritual of the First Plowing, a state ceremony of ancient Indian origin and uniquely Thai characteristics.

Now the Lord of the Harvest chooses at random one of three *panungs,* or old-style Siamese sarongs, offered him by a Brahman priest, and wraps it around his body. It is the medium-length *panung,* and to all the assemblage this is an omen of normal rainfall for the coming year.

The conch shells sound again to begin the plowing, and a pair of oxen which have been specially blessed for this ritual start forward, pulling a red-and-gold ceremonial plow that curves gracefully skyward like a soaring serpent. As it furrows the earth, the plow is flanked by eight scarlet-suited attendants, followed by the Lord of the Harvest, a Brahman sprinkling lustral water on the ground, and four silk-clad Celestial Maidens tossing blessed rice seeds from gold and silver baskets. After a given area has been plowed, the sacred oxen are unyoked and led within reach of seven dishes that have been filled separately with rice, corn, beans, sesame seed, wine, water and grass. What will the animals choose? The first dish to be touched by one of the oxen contains wine, and this causes the Royal Astrologers present to predict on the spot that for the coming year Thailand will enjoy an abundance of rice, fruits and vegetables, as well as improved international trade and communications. The ceremony ends with the crowd dashing into the newly-plowed furrows to scoop up the sacred seeds, which they will mix with their own seeds at rice planting time to ensure a successful crop.

In the heart of Bangkok's fashionable Rajprasong district, a young Thai woman in chic Western dress walks into the front court of a modern luxury hotel, looks shyly around, and then approaches a concrete miniature house that stands on a pedestal in the courtyard. She puts several lighted incense sticks on the pedestal and kneels before it in prayer. This woman has recently been married, and she is praying to the spirit that dwells in the little house for a son. The spirit house, only a few yards removed from the bustle of 20th Century traffic, belongs to the hotel. But this particular spirit has been found so helpful by the Bangkok public that the shrine is daily inundated with fresh flowers, candles and burning incense brought by people who come in off the street.

The reverent observance of Visakha Bucha, the pageantry of the First Plowing, and the intimate praying of the young wife are each revealing in part of the spiritual makeup of the Thai people. In Thailand, religion is no fire and brimstone from the pulpit. It has little to do with the self-flagellation of the ascetic or the religiosity of the militant evangelist. It is rather a way of being and looking at the world — philosophical, mystical, sometimes baffling to the Westerner — that permeates every part of one's existence. Here not only life's major milestones such as birth, marriage and death are occasions for religious observances, but minor steps — the ground-breaking for a house, the installation of a new factory machine, the opening of a bowling alley — are all occasions for religious sentiment too. Each morning Thai women the country over wait patiently with their best food prepared for that single file of silent, saffron-robed monks carrying alms bowls. Most Thai young men expect to join the monkhood themselves for several weeks or several months at some point in their lives. A building in Thailand, whether a home, a factory, a hotel or a government office, normally has a Buddhist altar inside and a spirit house outside. Religion molds the forms, the shapes and the motifs of Thai architecture, sculpture, painting, literature and theater.

Buddhism is the state religion, but in Thailand, as in most other Far Eastern countries, natural tolerance and a lack of doctrinaire attitudes have resulted in a syncretism, or merging, of faiths, a process that seems very natural to everybody in this part of the world. Thai Buddhism is practiced in conjunction with a large number of Brahmanic rituals, and at the popular level is hopelessly entangled with animism, the worship of natural spirits.

Buddhism, which originated in India, arrived in what is now Thailand long before the Thais themselves did — in the Third Century B.C., according to Thai Buddhist scholars. The city of Nakorn Pathom, 30 miles west of Bangkok, was at that time the capital of the Indianized kingdom of Dvaravati, and from here orthodox, or Theravada Buddhism is believed to have spread. In a later era, Burmese conquerors in the North propagated the same faith. Simultaneously the Khmers brought their Angkor version of Hinduism into the area of the Chao Phraya River Valley. When the mainly animist Thais arrived from China, they adopted the local beliefs — so that Theravada Buddhism, tinged with leftover Hinduism and animism, became the state religion of the early Siamese kingdoms. Today nearly 94 percent of the people of Thailand are Theravada Buddhists. Less than two percent, mostly of Chinese origin, are Mahayana Buddhists — a variation of the same religion about which more will be said later. Moslems constitute some four percent of the total, while Christians number only about 150,000, or half of one percent of the Thai population, despite centuries of Western missionary efforts.

Popular opinion has it that human beings in Thailand are greatly outnumbered by an extramundane population of elves, pixies, demons, genies, ghouls, goblins, vampires, banshees and other assorted incorporeal entitles who are believed to spend their time abetting or generally messing up human activities. These astral beings, called *phis* (the word *phi* is pronounced like the letter P), are said to be domiciled in heaven, on earth and in hell. The earthly variety reside in houses, gardens, orchards, rice fields, trees, rivers, mountains, and in the bodies of people. Some do not have homes, and wander endlessly across the countryside.

The spirits must be propitiated with suitable gifts, because their help in an emergency can be invaluable and their hostility can be ruinous. They can be bribed, coerced and bamboozled. *Phis* have distinctive personalities; some are benevolent, others evil. They have been known to be phlegmatic, prankish, whimsical, gullible, greedy, lecherous or prudish. One has to learn about the temperament of the particular *phi* whose attention he is soliciting or getting rid of, or he will be in trouble.

In the yard of almost every home in Thailand is an object resembling a doll house or bird house, fixed to a wooden post at eye level. This is the *sala phra phum*, or the abode of Chao Thi, the guardian spirit of the main house. Best known of the *phis*, his species is relied upon to ward off harmful influences from the home. His favor is invoked during a family crisis, when moving to a new dwelling, or on the occasion of lodging an overnight guest. The spirit house is surrounded by a platform, normally cluttered with incense sticks, candles, flowers, sweets and — as a reward for granting special favors — miniature clay figures of dancing girls, horses or elephants, and perhaps a jug of rice whiskey. The *sala phra phum* must face north at a spot where the shadow of the main house never falls on it, or the spirit would refuse to take up residence. On the other hand, the shadow of the spirit house must never fall on the main house, in which resides the Buddha, a higher deity, who has his own altar and sometimes a special chapel. The Buddha and Chao Thi come from two different cosmoses, but they coexist amicably because the protocol-conscious Thais know how to demarcate their respective domains.

Besides the *phi* of one's individual house, there are *phis* of cities and of the country as a whole. The guardian spirit of Bangkok lives in a carved wooden post within a yellow stucco shrine called the Lak Muang, which is hidden behind an unsightly filling station. The shrine makes up for its small size and unpretentious location by the extreme effectiveness of its resident spirit in the minds of the populace. This *phi* not only guards the city but also serves as patron to the aficionados of games of chance. The Lak Muang is perpetually crowded with happy lottery winners and hopeful neophytes, and within its precincts the hawkers of lottery tickets often set up for business.

The guardian spirits of various domains are propitiated on regular occasions; thus the *phis* of the rice fields receive offerings at the time of plowing, sowing, transplanting and harvest. Some spirits that enter a person's body do so of their own accord, but many of the most helpful ones must be invited in and made to feel at home there with gifts and other attentions. A *phi meng* can cure a sick person. The *phi pokalong* is a kind of private eye, useful to help locate stolen objects and to identify thieves. A *kumarn thong,* or "golden child," the ghost of a stillborn baby, is especially welcome because he makes his keeper invulnerable to injury and warns him against thefts. Of a mischievous turn is the *phi buay;* when this spirit gets into a person, the latter acts normally in every way except that he or she refuses to wear any clothes.

Among the evil *phis* that trouble Thai country dwellers are the ghosts of people who died violent deaths or were improperly buried. And sometimes the spirit inside a living person may go berserk and be guilty of breaking out to commit harmful acts. Often professional help must be sought from an *acharn,* a villager with occult powers, who might get rid of a malevolent *phi* by adjuration — much in the manner of exorcising a possessed person in Europe of the Middle Ages — or the *acharn* might contrive to send the evil spirit away on a miniature raft downstream.

The galaxy of Thai spirits merges imperceptibly into the pantheon of Hindu gods whom the Thais took over from the ancient Khmers — a vast heavenly population of 330 million heroes, demons, sylphlike dancing girls and mythical animals. Hinduism, or Brahmanism, is not practiced as a distinct religion by the Thais. But most of the rites and ceremonies concerning national events, as well as family affairs like marriage and cremation, are of Brahmanic origin; and Hindu deities are worshipped side by side with the Buddha and the *phis.*

Hinduism originated in India more than 4,000 years ago. To the religion scholar it is a subtle and profound philosophy, the basic concept of which is the impermanence of the physical and the relentless recurrence of life. Popular Hinduism falls mainly into the cults of Vishnu and Siva, and much of the Khmer's Siva cult remains with the Thais. Although Siva is the god who destroys, the fact that death brings rebirth means that to Siva is attributed reproductive power; this is symbolized by the lingam, or phallic symbol, which was worshipped by the Khmers and is still to be found in many places in Thailand. The elephant-headed, multi-armed Ganesha, a son of Siva, is the patron of all Siamese arts.

The god Vishnu is best known to the Thais in the incarnation in which he is called Rama. The story of Rama is from the sacred Indian classic, the *Ramayana;* it was borrowed by the Thais, revised, embellished, and transmuted into the *Ramakien,* the great Thai epic that supplies the leitmotif for almost all Siamese art and literature. The basic plot is identical in both versions: Crown Prince Rama, unjustly exiled by his father, goes to the jungle accompanied by his devoted wife, Sita. She is later kidnapped by the demon-king, Tossakan, and taken to Ceylon. Rama raises an army and, with the help of Hanuman, the monkey god, he marches to Ceylon via a causeway built by monkeys, slays Tossakan and rescues Sita.

In the Royal Chapel at Bangkok, better known as the Temple of the Emerald Buddha, many of the Hindu deities can be recognized. The murals on the cloister wall surrounding the temple hall depict the story of the *Ramakien,* and the giant demon guards in the courtyard are characters from this epic. On the temple gables are carved scenes of Vishnu riding on his man-bird mount, the *garuda.* The roof of the Royal Pantheon in the temple is topped with the trident of Siva. Scattered about the temple grounds are gilded and stucco statues of *garudas, kinnaris* (half human, half bird, celestial musicians) and *norasinghs* (half human, half lion creatures) — all from the Hindu heavens.

But the most profound influence to reach Thailand from India was the philosophy of the man who came to be known in the ancient Sanskrit language of his day as the Buddha. Siddhartha Gautama was a prince born to a tribal chieftain in northern India, in what is now Nepal, about 563 B.C. His father lavished affection on the boy and made sure as he grew up that Siddhartha never had any first-hand knowledge of the pains and miseries that accompany human existence for most ordinary mortals. He was 29 years old and himself the father of a young son when Prince Siddhartha, riding one day through a poor village, was shocked to see a sick man, an old man and a dead man. His discovery of human suffering, and the terrible thought that one must repeat such suffering through endless rein-carnations — a concept he accepted like other Hindus — dis-turbed him so deeply that he resolved to devote the rest of his lifetime to a search for the meaning of it all. Renounc-ing his wealth and title, he left his family and went out into the world alone.

For six years he tried the fasting, self-mortification and other mystic exercises performed by ascetic Hindu holy men; his body was weakened, but he found himself no closer to an understanding of the meaning of life. He went to sit in the shade of a huge spreading tree, determined to meditate until the truth came to him. After many weeks of meditation, suddenly he saw it all clear. The cause of human suffering lies in man's own desires; man must con-trol his cravings for worldly pleasures in order to achieve spiritual serenity. To live is to suffer, and to be reborn is to suffer again. The only way to escape reincarnation and break the chain of suffering is by leading a life of perfect goodness and moderation, and thus to achieve Nirvana — an ineffable state of bliss in which all cravings disappear, the ego dies, and the individual is beyond pleasure or sor-row, good or evil, life or death.

The moment of insight that came to the young prince is called the Enlightenment. Siddhartha Gautama henceforth became the Buddha, or the Enlightened One. The tree under which he had meditated for so long became the Bodhi, or the Tree of Wisdom. The Buddha spent the remaining 45 years of his life traveling through India, preaching, arguing, and imparting his wisdom to the disciples who gathered about him in increasing numbers. His teachings constitute a whole system of rationalist philosophy, at the base of which is the postulate that every object, living being and state of affairs in the universe is constantly changing. These changes are brought about not by any divine being or supernatural force, but by *Karma,* the Law of Cause and Effect, which is impartial, impersonal, absolute and unchanging. Governed by the inexorable workings of the natural law, man can still act to decide his own salvation. The Buddha taught that each good or bad deed done by a person becomes a factor in determining that person's future state. At reincarnation, one suffers the consequences of past sins and enjoys the benefits of past virtues.

In terms of everyday morality, the Buddha taught that man should not lie, steal, commit adultery, indulge in intoxicants, or kill any living creature. His formula for human behavior was the gentle doctrine of brotherhood.

Soon after the Buddha's death a great schism developed among his followers, and Buddhism was split into two schools. The orthodox school adheres closely to the Buddha's original teaching, believes in salvation through individual effort, and uses the traditional Pali scriptures. It is known as Theravada Buddhism, or the Doctrine of the Elders, but is often referred to as Hinayana ("Lesser Vehicle") Buddhism, a somewhat disrespectful name invented by the breakaway school which calls its doctrine Mahayana ("Greater Vehicle") Buddhism. The Mahayanists favor a liberal interpretation of the Master's teachings and have added many new concepts, including salvation by grace, the existence of heaven and hell, and the partial sanctification of the Bodhi-sattvas, those persons already qualified for Nirvana who voluntarily choose to go through further incarnations in order to help others.

Eventually Theravadism took root in southern Asia in the lands of Ceylon, Burma, Thailand, Cambodia and Laos. Mahayanism became dominant in China, Korea, Japan and Vietnam. Among the various Mahayanist sects, Zen Buddhism, which emphasizes contemplation rather than discussion and preaching, is the most widespread and powerful, particularly in China and Japan. In Tibet and Mongolia, Mahayanism went through a process of mixture with native Shamanism to become Lamaism. In India, where the religion was born, Buddhism has all but disappeared, after an initial dominance over Hinduism.

Theravada Buddhism is, in a strict sense, a logical and intensely individualistic code of ethics rather than a religion. It offers nothing mystical or supernatural to invite mortal awe. The Buddha did not proclaim the existence of any deity, and he was not himself a god but a teacher. (With characteristic tolerance, however, the Buddha did not specifically deny the existence of the numerous gods, angels and spirits that peopled the Far Eastern cosmos in the popular mythology of his day as of ours.) The concept of a single, all-powerful Lord in Heaven, such as the God of the Judeo-Christian tradition, did not reach Southeast Asia until the monotheism of Islam arrived from India in the 14th Century — and most of the peoples of Malaysia, Indonesia and the Philippines accepted the Allah of Mohammed's teachings. Among the Thais, monotheism has never made much headway.

Buddhism may be defined by its purist practitioners as a rationalist — and indeed thoroughly agnostic — philosophy. But in Thailand, as elsewhere, Buddhism operates on more than one level. And on the popular level it is by any definition a great religion — with a vast canonical liturgy, a powerful and independent priesthood, and a huge body of devoted followers who find in the observance of temple rites and other manifestations of their faith a strong emotional satisfaction. In Thailand, throngs of worshippers crowd into tens of thousands of temples on *Wan Phra*, the Buddhist Sunday (it falls on the eighth and fifteenth day of the waxing and waning moon) ; and on all the days in between, reverent individuals are to be found visiting the temples, filling these holy places with fragrant flowers and incense, and plastering gold foil on countless Buddha images.

Such activities are manifestations of *tam boon*, or making merit. While the great goal of Buddhists is to attain Nirvana, this is recognized as a very difficult thing to do, and only a monk has much chance of success in the foreseeable future. The more immediate and practical concern of most ordinary Buddhists is to improve themselves — and thus move closer to that ultimate state of bliss — while going through the cycles of rebirth. Merit-making is like storing up credits in the heavenly ledger; it improves one's chances in the next life. To be born a prince, perhaps, instead of a poor peasant, or a mighty elephant instead of a lowly pig.

But this is not all. Thoughtful Buddhists point out that the practice of merit-making instills in the individual a sense of sacrifice, while directing him toward acts of generosity and loving kindness. A person can gain merit by freeing captured birds and fish, by being charitable to the poor, by listening to sermons, reciting scriptures, worshipping at the temple, feeding the monks and gilding Buddha images. Every king of Thailand sponsors the erection and renovation of *wats* as a potent, high-level method of making merit.

Of Thailand's present 23,700 *wats*, 159 are royal establishments built and maintained by the crown. The remainder are supported by the general population, who regularly contribute an estimated one tenth of their income for this purpose without the necessity of any subscription or campaign for funds. In addition, communities provide voluntary labor for the construction of temples and other religious structures. The humblest Thai village has at least one *wat,* while Bangkok has nearly 400. *Wats* vary in size and wealth from single-room shrines to great monasteries with dozens of resplendent temple halls, pagodas and pavilions, their precincts filled with hundreds of Buddha images and demon gate-keepers. The *wat* is the most important community center in every village. Customarily it is not only the place to worship and seek spiritual solace, but also a seat of learning, a book depository, a wayfarers' inn, local club house, bank vault, and the site of innumerable country fairs and festivals.

Most *wats* of any size have a number of cells for resident monks, and one or more school buildings. Education in Thailand used to be entirely the responsibility of the monkhood; although the Thai government now directs a national education program, more than half of the *wats* still maintain their classrooms. Temple courtyards are usually covered with sand, brought by local people as ·a form of merit-making at religious festivals — a useful devotional gesture in a land of seasonal floods, as the sand raises the temple grounds above surrounding areas. Main temple halls always face east, because the Buddha sat facing the east under the Bodhi tree at his Enlightenment. Almost every *wat* has a big, sacred Bodhi tree, grown from a cutting either from the original tree in India or from one of its descendants in Ceylon.

Each *wat* harbors between one and several hundred Buddha images, which may be made of plaster, stone, wood, crystal, jasper, ivory, terra cotta, bronze or gold. Buddha images were invented in India five centuries after the Buddha's death. Before that time there were only symbolic "reminders" to give Buddhists a continuing awareness of their great teacher: the Bodhi tree; the sacred serpent, which shielded the Buddha from the weather during his long meditation; the Wheel of Doctrine commemorating his first sermon; and the Buddha's bodily relics — bones, teeth, hair — which are buried here and there throughout the Buddhist world in earth mounds or piles of masonry called stupas, or pagodas, or *chedis*.

Buddha images are worshipped by Buddhists on all levels in Thailand. The rationalists see themselves as simply paying due homage to the Master; the reverence shown to teachers in the Orient is never quite distinct from worship. Others kneel before the images in the conviction that they are an extension of the Buddha himself, who is inaccessible because he has entered Nirvana.

A new Buddha image is regarded as an inanimate object until a particular Brahmanic ritual has been performed, after which it is considered alive. Buddha images are addressed with a special vocabulary. Countless miniature ones are fashioned in metal and terra cotta to be worn around the neck as charms, or sealed inside giant *chedis* to supercharge the latter spiritually. A few Buddha images, according to Thai lore in these matters, have been known to act destructively, bringing diseases, fires or earthquakes. But most are benign and protective. It is taken for granted in Thailand that every home, every city and every state needs a Buddha image to look after its welfare. Until recently a major duty of Thai kings and princes was to insure the safety of the patron images of their domains, and to rescue them if they were stolen or kidnapped.

Tales of Buddha images are woven all through the fabric of Thai history and tradition. In 1438 the Jinaraja Buddha of Sukhothai was reportedly seen to shed tears of blood during the visit of the Crown Prince of Ayudhya, which had just conquered Sukhothai. Around the turn of the century a giant reclining Buddha in Ang Thong province is said to have startled the monks of the monastery with a verbal warning of a cholera epidemic impending — and a prescription against the disease that worked.

In the historic city of Chiengmai repose three highly-prized Buddha images. In Wat Chiengmun sits a fake Buddha Sila, a bas-relief in stone; the genuine one, which originated in 13th-Century Ceylon, is locked in the abbot's quarters for fear of theft. It is taken out only to be used in processions for rain-making. Resting in the same monastery, and also believed useful as a rain-maker, is the Crystal Buddha. Once the patron of the city-state of Lampun, this image was captured by the King of Chiengmai in the 13th Century. Two centuries later a prince from Ayudhya went to the Chiengmai monastery, ostensibly to serve as a monk. When he left, he smuggled the sacred Buddha image to his home kingdom. This touched off what might well be called the "War of the Crystal Buddha," for the irate King of Chiengmai fought his way into Ayudhya, rescued the image and bore it back to Chiengmai, where it still remains.

Stories of Buddha images come right down to modern times. In 1955 a giant plaster image was being moved into a new temple hall in Bangkok's Wat Trimitr. It had sat in a shed for two decades in the monastery courtyard after being rescued from an abandoned temple near the harbor. The crane hook lifting the Buddha suddenly broke and the image fell to the ground, where it had to be left overnight through a thunderstorm. Next morning the abbot was cleaning the rain-soaked image when he noticed a metallic glint through some cracks in the plaster. He shelled off some of the plaster and found gold underneath. Upon removing all of the plaster, the monks discovered that they had a 19-karat gold Buddha, ten feet tall and weighing five and a half tons. The 13th-Century Gold Buddha, now safely enclosed in a ferroconcrete temple, is believed to have been camouflaged with its coating of plaster at the time of the Burmese invasions some 200 years ago.

For a Thai layman, to serve for a period as a Buddhist monk is both a devotional act and an important way to make merit. The length of service might vary from one week to several years. Some men, after joining, remain in the monkhood for life. The most usual practice is for a man upon reaching the age of 21 to become a monk for three months during the Buddhist Lent, which coincides with the rainy season. Thus membership in the order is in constant flux, with seasonal swellings between sowing and harvest. Normally Thailand has more than 150,000 *bhikkhus,* or full-fledged monks, and some 90,000 *samaneras,* or novice monks. They wear regulation, orange-yellow robes and are collectively called the Sangha, or the Brotherhood. The Sangha, which has complete independence in religious matters, is governed by a Sangha Supreme Council roughly paralleling the state Council of Ministers. Not members of the Sangha but a part of the religious establishment are some 2,000 white-robed *chees,* or nuns. These are devoted lay women, often aged and homeless, for whom separate nunneries are provided. Serving as page boys to the monks are 120,000 *dekwats,* or temple boys, who get their lodging and board at the monasteries.

The ordination of a novice monk is marked by a typical mixture of Brahmanic ritual, Buddhist prayer and Siamese festiveness. In preparation for monkhood the young man will have his hair and eyebrows shaved off. The last night before ordination is spent singing, dancing, drinking, and making merry with family, neighbors and friends. Early the next morning the whole crowd troops to the monastery in a procession, with banners, flowers, incense and gifts to the temple. The novitiate, dressed in an embroidered white robe and a pagoda hat like a dunce cap, and shielded by a colorful silk parasol, either rides on a horse or more often is jounced along on the shoulders of a husky neighbor, who jests with the others amid general laughter and music provided by the village band.

Inside the *wat,* the novitiate is handed over to the monks, sometimes after a theatrical bit of parrying with a man disguised as Mara the Tempter, who tries unsuccessfully to prevent the novitiate from entering the monastery. The young man is solemnly interrogated by the officiating monk to make sure that he is no fugitive from such mundane obligations as the military draft, or from an impatient creditor or angry wife. Upon acceptance, there is a chanting of scriptures, and the novitiate changes his white robe for the yellow robe of the Sangha.

The life of a Buddhist monk in Thailand is austere but not harshly ascetic. He gets up before sunrise at the sound of a drum, says his prayers, washes, sweeps his cell and courtyard, and filters his drinking water through a piece of cloth to make sure that he will not kill an insect by unwittingly swallowing it. As the sun peeps over the horizon, he marches outside with his colleagues in single file, each man carrying an alms bowl for food. By this time housewives are waiting to heap the bowls with rice curries, fish, vegetables and fruits, which the monks accept in silence and with downcast eyes. Giving to a monk is an act of merit-making, and the donor thanks the monk for accepting the food. If the monk should thank the donor, he would be robbing that person of his or her due merit. There is no doubt in the mind of a proper Buddhist that "it is better to give than to receive."

Back in the monastery, the monk pushes back his robe, baring one shoulder, and eats his first meal of the day. The second meal must be taken before noon, as only liquids are allowed after that time. Both mornings and afternoons are taken up by an hour or two of study or listening to a lecture, followed by a free period during which family and friends are permitted to visit. After the evening service the monk has another free period. Monasteries in Thailand are not cloisters, shutting their occupants away from the world. A daily stream of gregarious lay Buddhists enter the *wats* to worship, pray, listen to the scriptures, leave their valuables for safekeeping, seek personal advice or perhaps an herb remedy from the abbot, or just to gossip with the monks.

For the Sangha there are a total of 227 rules of conduct, but a novice is required to observe only ten. These include the standard Buddhist injunctions not to kill, steal, lie, or drink alcohol, and special prohibitions against handling money or engaging in sexual activity of any kind. For serious infractions of the rules, a monk is tried by a group of his brethren appointed by the Sangha Supreme Council, and if found guilty may be defrocked. There are very few cases of discipline, however, because the system has built-in safety valves. No one ever pressures a man to be a monk, in the first place; if an individual joins the Sangha, whether for a week or a lifetime, he does so because he genuinely wants to. Any time he grows weary of the monastic life he is free to leave as easily as he entered it. A novice can simply remove his monk's robe and declare: "I wish to leave the Sangha," and he is a layman again. A *bhikkhu* must go through a small ceremony involving his fellow monks and say: "I hereby take leave of the Sangha; may you all remember me as a layman." Then he departs, sprinkled by the monks with lustral water and blessings as he goes.

CHAPTER 4

An Ancient Heritage of Art

GODS levitate, demons hiss, mortals writhe and posture on the stone freizes of the great Hindu temples of India. Huge against a Cambodian sky stand the corncob towers of Angkor Wat, where topless Khmer princesses danced a millennium ago. Jewel-like pavilions with gold-tiled roofs and lacquered doors scintillate and coruscate beneath the sun in the Forbidden City of Peking. In a hundred thousand sanctuaries, across half a continent, the Buddha smiles his enigmatic smile.

Give these pervading cultural elements to an aesthetically sensitive, religiously devout, temperamentally exuberant people, living in a land of bursting blossoms and gaudy jungle birds. The result is traditional Thai art.

The art of Thailand is to an overwhelming degree religious in character. Inspiration for early Thai craftsmen came from many geographical quarters, but basically the influences can be seen as Indian and Chinese. Indianized peoples had lived in what is now Thailand for more than a thousand years before the Thais arrived in force in the Chao Phraya Valley in the 13th Century. The new arrivals found and took over elements in the Hindu-Buddhist cultures of the Mons of Dvaravati, the Srivijayans of Sumatra, and the Khmers of Cambodia. Just at this time the cultural influence of China was greatly expanded in Southeast Asia by the conquests of its Mongol emperors. As a result of contact with Peking, the Thais of the Sukhothai period incorporated many Chinese features into the arts of the new kingdom. Borrowing thus from many sources, Thai craftsmen achieved their own artistic synthesis — a synthesis in which racial characteristics and physical environment acted together with cultural osmosis to determine a unique national style.

The Sukhothai era (1238-1350) is the Golden Age of Thai art. Western connoisseurs believe that some of the carved Buddha images of this period must be ranked among the finest of all religiously-inspired works of man. In contrast to the elaborate ornamentation employed in many other national art forms, the early Thai sculptors portrayed the human figure with utmost simplicity. During the ensuing Ayudhya era (1350-1767) Thai artisans concentrated on decorative beauty, producing splendid, polychromatic buildings, fancifully carved teak doors, rococo lacquerware, elaborately inlaid mother-of-pearl furniture, and gorgeous court and theatrical costumes. Unhappily, the taste for decoration became gluttonous, and by the start of the Bangkok era in the late 18th Century many new buildings were mere showpieces of architectural finery, and even Buddha images were sometimes encrusted with cheap gems. This artistic degeneration is deplored by thoughtful people in today's Thailand, many of whom seek a renaissance of classical aesthetic values — meaning particularly a return to the serene simplicity shown in the work of the Sukhothai era.

The earliest known Buddha images were made in India in the 1st Century B.C. by the Graeco-Buddhist school of Gandhara. But it was the Gupta style, bulky and round, emerging in India after several centuries of development, that became adopted by most of the other peoples of Asia, including the Mons and the Khmers. These precursors of the Thais carved the images in stone, like most Buddhist artisans in Southeast Asia before the 12th Century. The Thais, however, have historically made very few stone images, preferring to work with stucco or bronze. Bronze casting, learned from either the Chinese or the Indians, made possible a distinctive Thai school of Buddhist sculpture. The full, round, Gupta features of the Indian, Mon and Khmer images, so natural to stone carving, can be seen in the early Thai bronzes of the Northern, or Chiengsan, school. But by the 14th Century the magnificent Sukhothai school had created a more delicate, emotive style.

The technique used, in which the features of an image are modeled in wax, is known as the *cire perdu,* or "lost wax," method of bronze casting. As practiced by the Sukhothai sculptors, first an inner mold is made with a mixture of clay, rice husk and cow dung — a secret of success, for this mixture does not shrink or expand at high temperature. The inner mold is covered with a layer of wax, on which the actual sculpting is done by the artist. This work is then covered with an outer mold. Now the whole thing is heated to melt and drain off the wax through holes left in the base. The space formerly occupied by the wax is filled with a liquid bronze alloy. After cooling, the outer mold is broken away to reveal the finished bronze figure.

For Buddha images, tradition decrees only four acceptable postures: sitting, standing, reclining or walking. There are three accepted ways of crossing the legs for the sitting position, and some half dozen hand gestures to signify various activities such as "meditating," "dispelling fear," and "victory over Mara, the Tempter." A distinct innovation of Sukhothai artisans is the three-dimensional walking Buddha; this difficult posture was attempted by the Indians only in bas-relief. The Sukhothai walking Buddha depicts the Great Teacher after his Enlightenment, stepping forth gently to deliver his doctrine to the world. It conveys to the viewer the same feeling of tranquillity as the sitting Buddha, but with the added sense of movement and a complete harmony of fluid lines. Viewed from the side, the shoulders of the walking Buddha are exaggerated in contour — an exaggeration which gives a roundness most pleasing to the eye when the figure is enshrined in a niche, as intended, and viewed from the front.

The traditional artist of Thailand is anonymous, for his aim is to glorify the Buddha, not himself, and to make merit, not money. He may be a scholarly monk, a devout layman, or a professional craftsman. He is deliberately unoriginal, for he seeks the perfection of a time-honored mode of expression rather than the innovation of something unique. However, even confined within the bounds of tradition, he sometimes — perhaps unwittingly — manages to stamp his work with marks of individual creativity.

Many of the features found on Buddha images have been stylized for centuries. From descriptions of the living Gautama in the Pali scriptures Thai artists have been led to show the familiar protuberance atop the skull, the elongated ear-lobes, the spiraling curls of hair, very long arms, flat soles and projecting heels. From later poets of India have come the concepts of a head "with the shape of an egg," a chin "like a mango-stone," eyebrows "like drawn bows," and hands together "like a budding lotus." Although conventionalized in this manner, the Buddha images made by the Sukhothai sculptors exude a special serenity and spiritual force that is felt even by non-Buddhists. The body of the Sukhothai Buddha is delineated with soft and sinuous lines. A slightly full bosom and complete absence of muscle bulges make the figure look almost feminine. This effect is said to be deliberate; according to Buddhist belief, once a person achieves Nirvana it is meaningless to say whether he is alive or dead, much less to draw a distinction between masculine and feminine. Characteristic of the transcendental art of the East, a Buddha image does not really show the person of the Buddha, but is a personification of Buddhism itself.

The Sukhothai style of Thai sculpture evolved in the course of history into the Ayudhya, or National, style. This is a joining together of a number of earlier styles that fails to attain the great spirituality of the Sukhothai school. Toward the end of the Ayudhya period, sculpture had degenerated considerably as a consequence of the growing passion for decorative finery. During the massive rehabilitation of the early Bangkok era (*circa* 1800), great efforts were made by kings and commoners alike to salvage Buddha images from the ruined *wats* all over the war-torn country. King Rama I had no fewer than 1,200 bronze images brought by flotillas of colorful barges to Bangkok. In subsequent years, copies of some of the most sacred of the old Buddhas have been made in Thailand. But as far as new work is concerned, the art of Buddha sculpture had died out by the last quarter of the 19th Century.

Contrasting with the simplicity of line of traditional Thai sculpture is the rich complexity of Thai wood carving. The popularity once enjoyed by this art form is understandable in the land of teak, which is soft enough for the knife and yet not too palatable to termites. While wooden Buddhas are inferior and few in number in Thailand, wooden figures of mythical beings such as *garudas* and *kinnaris* by early craftsmen show a lively creativity and primitive charm. Decorative carving was once done profusely on thrones, palanquins, elephant howdahs, royal barges, cremation floats, pavilions, pulpits, furniture, gables and doors. This traditional work sometimes represents mythical figures, and is sometimes composed of stylized floral patterns or tracery designs. The carving always fills up the entire space available, and is normally coated with lacquer or gilt. Fine examples in temples and public buildings must be preserved as part of a vanishing artistic heritage, for today the art of wood carving in Thailand is virtually extinct.

A combination of damp, tropical climate and Burmese invasions has left in existence only a very few Thai paintings dating back to the great period before the 18th Century — mostly temple murals. Lineal and two-dimensional in character, these paintings were done with subtle earth pigments to produce an effect midway between chiaroscuro and polychromy. The murals in the *bot* of Wat Sutat are considered very fine examples of a classic Thai style, but those in the gallery of the Temple of the Emerald Buddha, often visited by tourists, are an unfortunate modern restoration, vulgarized by bright chemical pigments and an intrusion of Western perspective.

Of all the fine arts, architecture in Thailand provides the best illustration of the manner in which cultural borrowing, a penchant for the indigenous, and the availability of materials have combined to determine a national style. Thai architects of the Sukhothai kingdom had as their first models the monochromatic Khmer temples, which have roofs of horizontal stone slabs with a cylindrical dome in the center. The Thais built their roofs of teakwood, which was far more plentiful than stone in the area of the Chao Phraya Valley, and in the course of time Thai builders gave

the roofs a very different shape. The steep, slightly con-
cave temple roofline admired by so many visitors to the
country is that of the ordinary thatched roof of a Thai
dwelling weighed down with tropical rainwater. Thus has
a functional defect been turned into an aesthetic delight.

To roof over a very large building without having it
look top-heavy, the Thai builders employed the many-tiered
roof, which gives a sense of rhythm and mobility to an
otherwise ponderous structure. The effect of movement is
accentuated by slender, curvaceous *chofas,* or finials, soaring from ridge ends. (The *chofa* is a device that may have
had its origin in the horns of Indonesian spirit carvings.)
The *nagas,* or sacred serpents, found on the stone gables
of the Khmer temples were adopted by the Thais, but were
delicately carved in wood, with undulating forms and sky-
pointing tails. The Sukhothai kings, who maintained close
cultural relations with China, introduced many Chinese
characteristics into Thai architecture, including colored
roofing tiles and gilt ornamentation. The Thais took enthu-
siastically to the use of color, and later construction in the
country embodied more and more brilliant decoration.
Sometimes a brick building would be encrusted with countless pieces of broken Chinese porcelain to achieve a jewel-
like surface effect. Such extravagance of ornamentation
gives a make-believe, fairyland quality to much of Thai
architecture as viewed by the visitor today. At sunset the
great temples and palaces, their gables bordered with
gilded teak *nagas* and often studded with dazzling bits of
colored glass or porcelain, are like bouquets of brilliant
flowers amid the green foliage of their tropical surroundings.

Traditional Thai architecture can best be observed in
a typical *wat,* or temple compound. Every *wat* has a *bot,*
a temple hall enshrining the main Buddha image, where
the monks worship and meditate. This is normally a rec-
tangular wooden building having a steep roof built in mul-

tiple tiers and covered with glazed tiles. Most *wats* have a *viharn,* which is a temple hall housing numerous other images where laymen do their worshipping. The *bot* and the *viharn* are architecturally similar, but the former may be recognized by the fact that it is always surrounded by eight symbolic boundary stones. Temple halls are usually enclosed by a rectangle of galleries with elaborate gateways.

A third typical religious building is the *chedi,* originally the most sacred of structures because it enshrined relics of the Buddha, but now a general Buddhist symbol like the Christian cross. The classical Thai *chedi* is directly inspired by the Ceylonese stupa and its Indian prototype. It consists of a drumlike base supporting a bell-shaped dome, above which is a cubicle enclosing the throne of the Buddha and a slender pinnacle symbolic of a many-tiered umbrella. The graceful outline of the *chedi* is everywhere to be seen in Thailand. Built of brick and masonry, whitewashed or gilded, *chedis* range from miniatures of a few feet in height to the 380-foot giant in Nakorn Pathom.

Another type of stupa is the more massive *prang,* shaped exactly like a corncob, as exemplified by the corner towers of Angkor Wat and other Khmer temples. The Temple of the Emerald Buddha has eight big *prangs* representing the eight preceding reigns of the Chakri Dynasty. The best known and most monumental *prang* in Thailand is the 243-foot tower of the Temple of the Dawn. This porcelain-encrusted, pyramid-like structure overlooks the Chao Phraya River in Thonburi, and looms on the Bangkok horizon as the most notable tourist sight of Thailand.

Although some buildings in a *wat* may be added at random from time to time, the *bot, viharn* and *chedi* are always placed in a harmonious relationship one to another. Viewed from the air, the horizontal masses of temple buildings are effectively balanced by the vertical lines of the *chedis* and the *prangs.* Among numerous other religious buildings that may be seen in a temple compound are the *mondop,* a smallish, cube-shaped brick structure surrounded by pillars and topped with a crown-like wooden roof of many receding stories ending in a slender pinnacle. It is used to enshrine sacred objects. Serving either a religious or secular function is the *prasat,* a building with a Greek-cross plan and a typical Thai roof surmounted by either a *prang* or a crown-shaped pinnacle. The *prasat* in the Temple of the Emerald Buddha is the Royal Pantheon, containing statues of all the Chakri kings. Other structures to be found in a typical *wat* include the library for housing sacred books, the belfry, and a variety of small pavilions.

Much less Indianized than other elements of its culture is the language of Thailand. By internal structure and vocabulary, Thai belongs to the Sinitic (that is, Chinese) linguistic group. It is basically monosyllabic and has a vast number of homonyms, or words of identical sound but different meaning. To differentiate the homonyms one uses a variety of tones, five in standard Thai but seven in some dialects. The language is uninflected — which is to say that words do not change to show distinctions of case, gender, number or tense — and there are no varying grammatical endings. Every word is self-contained and unmodifiable. It may be a noun, an adjective, a verb or an adverb, depending on its position in a sentence; there are no articles, prepositions or conjunctions. Thus, as explained by a language expert at Chulalongkorn University in Bangkok, if one wants to say, "a big black dog chases a small white cat and bites it," in Thai this will be: "dog black body big run chase bite cat white body small."

Greatly complicating the monosyllabic, non-inflectional Thai is a borrowing of vocabulary from the polysyllabic and inflectional Sanskrit and Pali languages. In adopting new words, the Thais have had no compunction about telescoping or sloughing off syllables which they dislike or find difficult to pronounce. The two well-known Bangkok streets, Patpongse and Suriwongse, are pronounced with a silent "se," and the name of the god Indra is pronounced simply "Ind." Sanskrit and Pali words have enriched the Thai vocabulary considerably, and their use is to some extent a mark of upper-class status in Thailand. There is a formal vocabulary for writing, public speaking and radio broadcasting, as distinguished from the words normally used in conversation. And special vocabularies have been developed for use at the royal court, for addressing the Buddha, and for such ritual endeavors as elephant hunting.

The Thai alphabet, instituted by King Rama Kamheng of Sukhothai, and modeled after old Khmer and Indian alphabets, has 44 consonants, 24 vowels and four tonal signs. The vowels are written as separate signs above, below, before or after the consonants. The writing runs from left to right in a continuous flow, without any punctuation.

Besides using tricky tones and illogically skipping over Indian syllables, the Thais have several bewildering ways of rendering their language into English. The process can be based on phonetics, on the transliteration of Thai words, or on the transliteration of words from Sanskrit or Pali. Most Thais and resident foreigners now use a mixed system which might have been designed to drive the uninitiated to insanity. For example, the name for the city of Sawankaloke is not only spelled with several minor variations of the letters used here (i.e., Sawankalok, Sawonkalok), but is also Romanized as Svargaloka and Sajjanalaya. Many outsiders pronounce Thailand correctly as *tieland*, but few realize in reading Romanized Thai words that the *h* in *ph, dh* and *th* is silent; *b* and *v* are pronounced *p* and *w* respectively; *j* at the end of a syllable is pronounced *t;* and *l* in a similar position sounds like *n*. Thus the king's name, Bhumibol Adulyadej, should be pronounced *pumipon adoonyadet*. In short, there is no easy way for the foreigner to learn Thai without tears — even in the Land of Smiles.

The Thai language, although not suited to technological usage, is a tremendous vehicle for conveying ordinary meanings through the play of words, because it is full of titillating puns and *double entendres*. Thai literature, which makes copious use of rhyming and alliteration, existed mainly in verse form before the mid-19th Century — a collection of mythological epics of ancient origin, intended for recitation. Today the Thai classics, strict in meter and rich with Sanskrit and Pali words, are read only by intellectuals. A more popular form of literature is the folk tale in simple verse, based on one of the old epic poems, which is intoned by monks and learned laymen at *wat* festivals. Some of these tales — recited, sung and dramatized by itinerant minstrels and actors for centuries — have been so embellished that, despite their religious origin, they have become profane. The legends have inspired a great number of modern stories of romance and adventure in loose verse, designed to be read aloud. They are interminable melodramas concerned with noble heroes who, by supernatural powers and derring-do, are able to conquer impregnable cities and distaff hearts with equal ease. These romantic stories — always with a happy ending — have a strong hold on the sentimental Thais.

The theatre in Thailand weaves together the arts of music, dancing and drama. Thai music sounds monotonous and strange to the Western ear; unlike Western music, it has a scale of seven full tones evenly spaced within an octave, no half tones, and no system of harmony. The music is played in simple double time, and with little variation in intensity. Its beauty lies solely in the embellishment of a basic air. Musicians traditionally learn the melody by ear, then supply a sort of impromptu, original embroidery each time they play.

The Thais have some 50 different musical instruments, with percussives predominant. In a typical small ensemble, or *pipat* band, the melody is supplied by the *gong wong yai,* a set of 16 gongs suspended in a nearly circular rack around the player. Its crisp, brassy sound is overlaid by the staccato tones of the *ranad ek,* a xylophone of seasoned hardwood or bamboo in the shape of a Thai river boat. The only non-percussion instrument in a small ensemble is the oboe-like *pinai,* which is an old device that sounds like the Scotch bagpipe and is played like it — except that the player uses his cheeks instead of a windbag. He has to supply a continuous stream of forced air with his mouth to make the *pinai* shriek and grunt, even while inhaling. A small band usually has in addition a *tapone,* which is a double-ended hand timpano of Indian origin, and a pair of Chinese drums, the *klong thad,* which emit a sonorous *toom-toom-tom.* A Thai band has no conductor; time is kept for everybody by the player of the *ching,* or small cymbals.

Big orchestras in Thailand have many additional pieces, including stringed instruments. The best-loved of these is the ancient *saw sam sai,* a fiddle made of a triangular coconut shell, an ivory stem and three silk strings. A renowned *saw sam sai* player was King Rama II; he was so enthusiastic about it that he exempted from taxation all plantations growing the triangular coconuts. The popularity of this instrument has been reinforced recently by its exposure on television. Another traditional Thai stringed instrument is the *chakhay,* a thick-stemmed guitar played on a low table, almost always by a woman. Mainstays of the large orchestra include two Chinese-style fiddles, the *saw duang* and the *saw oo,* whose sighing sounds are also considered ideal for the often-heard solos of lament.

Thai melodies with Western-style harmony first appeared in the late 19th Century when, at a gala ball honoring the visiting Crown Prince of Russia, a military band played a "Quadrille on Siamese Airs." Since then, numerous attempts at hybridization have been made, some more successful than others. Today many young Thais are learning to play Western instruments. The most celebrated of such musicians, an accomplished saxophonist and composer of jazz medleys, is the currently reigning King Bhumibol.

Dancing in Thailand is just as much a part of everyday life as music. The national folk dance, called the *ramwong,* can be seen at country festivals, where all the villagers join in. It looks like a cross between a shy, slow cha-cha-cha and a disjointed Greek *karagouna,* but has a flavor all its own. In addition to the *ramwong,* which is loved by Thais everywhere, there are many regional folk dances. The most famous of these is the dreamy *fawn lep,* or nail dance, of Chiengmai. It is best done by the beauteous, fair-skinned Northern belles, who wear long, pointed metal extensions of fingernails to make their hands look like slender-petaled orchids. The sultry and coquettish mood of this dance contrasts strongly with the angularity and force of classical Thai dancing.

Classical dancing, which is the basic and essential element in a classical theatre performance in Thailand, is a heritage from ancient Bengal and Madras, handed down via medieval Angkor and Palembang. Today this art has completely died out in India, and there are only traces of it left in Indonesia; the Cambodians, who lost it once, borrowed back the classical dance form from the Thais in the 19th Century. The great French sculptor, Auguste Rodin, once saw a Paris performance by Cambodian dancers who had re-learned the forgotten art from Thai teachers. He exclaimed: "They have found postures which I had not dreamed of, movements which were unknown to us even in ancient times."

The movements are stylized and disciplined — a choreography of symbolic postures and gestures so difficult to perfect that the performers must be trained from childhood. As evolved in Thailand, the repertoire in this type of theatrical presentation is confined almost entirely to well-known episodes from the *Ramakien*. Men in embroidered costumes strike heroic poses as the legendary King Rama and his brother, Lakshama. Others in fantastic masks dance in loutish steps as demons, or skittish jumps as monkeys, while sloe-eyed actresses mince flirtatiously in brocaded gowns, clinking anklets, and pagoda-shaped coronets. Legs are flexed, arms outstretched, and fingers bent backwards in precise, well-controlled movements, creating a theatrical kaleidoscope in which one polychromatic tableau dissolves into another. The costume is as rich and elaborate as Thai architecture. (In contrast, there is an almost total absence of stage props.) Tradition dictates not only the detailed movements of the dance, but also the specific accompanying music. There are tunes for walking, fighting, weeping and love-making. By just listening to the music outside the theatre, a stage buff in Thailand can tell exactly what is going on within.

The earliest form of dance-drama known to the Thais, an art now virtually extinct, is the *nang*, or shadow-play. Introduced from the Indonesian empire of Srivijaya, the *nang* was performed behind a lighted screen with elaborately shaped cowhide figures depicting characters from the *Ramakien* and other classical romances. To the accompaniment of orchestral music, choral singing, and the words of a narrator, each player carried a figure on two sticks, moving it about behind the screen, on which recognizable shadows would come alive. Thai scholars believe that the motions and footwork of these shadow-players grew into a stylized dance, and this dance eventually became the *khon*, or masked drama, one of the principal forms of classical Thai theatre.

All *khon* players are male. Except for those who play female roles, they wear grotesque masks as heroes, demons and monkeys. Different characters in the dance-drama are recognizable by the expressions of these masks. There are more than 30 varieties of simian masks and more than 100 varieties of demonic masks. As most *khon* players have masks completely covering their heads — making it difficult for them to speak lines — they pantomime and dance to the music, leaving the dialogue entirely to a narrator.

A more popular form of classical Thai theatre is the *lakorn* dance-drama, originally performed by all-male casts, later by all-female casts, and now very often by mixed theatrical groups. In the *lakorn*, only non-human characters wear masks; the dialogue is usually spoken by the players themselves, but is sometimes sung by a chorus. The *lakorn* differs substantially from the *khon* in that it emphasizes graceful instead of strenuous movements.

Classical acting, for either *khon* or *lakorn* players, is a lifetime occupation, demanding not only talent but long training and unceasing practice. The players, who start their schooling at about the age of six, must be typecast from the very beginning in one of four categories — man, woman, demon and monkey — according to individual build, bodily movement and personality. The roles of demon and monkey, always played by males, require especially arduous drills to repeat vigorous, acrobatic movements until these become second nature.

Boys and girls beginning their terpsichorean careers are taught to move their heads, bodies, limbs and fingers in rhythm with their own verbal simulation of music — which might sound like "phring phring phring, tup patup, phring phring tup," or perhaps "cha chong cha, thing chong thing." Only after concentrating on such monotonous routines for six months or a year are they allowed to practice the more intricate Alphabet of the Dance. There are 68 separate movements in this alphabet, with picturesque names such as: "the bee caressing the flower," "the stag walking in the forest," "the vine entwines the tree," and "Narai hurls his discus."

Classical Thai drama was once staged only in palaces, as the nobility provided its exclusive patrons. Today, *khon* and *lakorn* performances draw a somewhat wider audience in city theatres. But the type of dance-drama that appeals most to common folk everywhere in Thailand is the *likay,* a vulgarized form of *lakorn* with a repertoire from Sanskrit and Chinese historical romances as well as the *Ramakien*. This theatre-of-the-people is characterized by broad farce and earthy dialogue, with generous ad-libbing — sometimes in a bawdy vein — by the players. It is performed in *wats* and village squares, to the great relish and loud guffaws of the villagers.

After many generations of elaboration upon earlier forms, the fine arts in Thailand began to atrophy in the 19th Century. The situation was caused very largely by the onslaught of Western influence. Instead of pouring revenue into the *wats* in traditional fashion, the monarchy devoted more and more of the nation's wealth to railroads, highways, postal services and other modern improvements. Increasingly, Thai youths of upper-class family were sent to Paris, London and Lausanne to be educated — and to bring back the way of the *farangs*. The resulting social and economic changes caused the arrest and often the abandonment of traditional artistic effort. The classical drama gave way to the modern stage, which in turn disappeared as leading stage players turned to the more lucrative business of acting before movie cameras. Ferroconcrete replaced teak as the favorite building material of architects. Modern living — even at the Thai tempo, which is considerably slower than that of the West — outmoded the time-consuming craft of wood-carving. Furniture of chrome and plastic took the place of tables and cabinets of lacquer and inlaid mother-of-pearl. Today automobiles and airplanes are showing up in temple murals, while factories are creeping into the historic ruins of Ayudhya — to the dismay of protesting traditionalists.

The effects of American-style advertising, of juke boxes and television serials, are now being debated in intellectual circles in Bangkok, where a single surviving tree on a modern boulevard is cherished as might be the last rose of summer. The whole trend toward Westernization of the country is regarded as a deplorable setback to the nation's culture by some — but others see it as preparing the way for a welcome transition toward new and meaningful art forms. Contemporary art in Thailand is amorphous in form and hesitant in movement, but there are encouraging signs of experimentation.

In the mushrooming art galleries of Bangkok, the visitor encounters a proliferation of contemporary sculpture and painting by youthful Thai artists. These works range from the realistic to the impressionistic, from abstract modern to Siamese primitive. While some are altogether Western except for their Thai signatures, others are imaginative creations that appear to be new flowers from old roots. Among the latter are landscapes and figures of endemic style in oil, tempera and water color, woodcuts of contemporary rural scenes executed with traditional flavor, and sculptured nudes that look modern, yet are idealized along classic Sukhothai lines.

Since living art is, and should be, a mirror of contemporary thought and experience, there is no reasonable argument why the work of today's craftsmen should look the same as that done in centuries past. On the other hand, for the modern Thai artist to succumb unthinkingly to the tenets of Western intellectualism is as unnatural as to be enslaved by the stereotyped approach of his progenitors. Whether contemporary artists in Thailand will go the way of the Japanese in compartmentalizing their work into separate schools of traditional and Western modern, or go the way of the Mexicans in synthesizing the two into something new and ethnically genuine, remains for the future to disclose. Given time and continued social and economic stability, the chances seem favorable that the aesthetically sensitive Thais will achieve a meaningful artistic fusion — and an art that is distinctively Thai modern.

A Study in Brilliant Contrast

THAILAND is a country of paradoxes. More than any other Asian nation except Japan it has invited modernization – rushing to get on with industrial development and the building of roads, dams and skyscrapers, its citizens reaching avidly for Western-style clothes and automobiles and television. And yet in many ways the Thais continue to honor and uphold tradition. There are 23,000 Buddhist temples in the country, and orange-robed monks are everywhere in evidence, a part of one's daily life. Art here is very largely stylized, its forms unchanged from ancient originals based on religious themes. In the North country, teak trees are still felled by trained elephants, while all over Thailand farmers can be seen cultivating their paddy fields behind plodding water buffaloes – as the people of this region did a thousand years ago. A land of stunning contrasts, Thailand offers to the color photographer some of the world's most arresting subject matter. The proof is set forth on the following pages.

A work elephant carrying its mahout lumbers out of the teak forest onto a road in Northern Thailand, where a pair of young Thais go zipping past on a motorcycle.

88

Thai dancers in ornate costumes portray the ancient story of the Ramakien. *Here King Rama* (left) *and his brother, Lakshama, ride off to war in a golden chariot.*

Dancers are dwarfed by the huge head of Hanuman, the monkey god. In the legend, he enlarged his body to form a bridge for Rama's army to cross an enemy moat.

93

Market women in sampans congregate at the floating produce center on the

klong, *or canal, at Thonburi, the site of the old capital near Bangkok.*

The **klongs** *extend miles inland across flat, rice-growing country, reaching*

to thatched farm houses that stand on stilts above the seasonal flood.

*Harvesting rice, the staple
food and principal export
of Thailand, farm workers
in broad-brimmed sun hats
gather the stalks into
neat bundles for threshing.*

*A Japanese ship unloads
cement at a Bangkok pier,
before taking on a cargo of
rice and other Thai products.
Berthing here are vessels
from all over the globe.*

Typifying the big-city bustle
which new building and
prosperity have brought to
Bangkok is motor traffic
swarming across an overpass
in the Pratunam District.

This view of a busy Bangkok
intersection shows the
B.O.A.C. building, which
houses a restaurant and night
club, and (in background)
the modern President Hotel.

The Siam Intercontinental Hotel, like others erected in recent years in Bangkok, has a swimming pool to provide luxurious recreation for visitors to the city.

*Outside the Temple of the Emerald Buddha in Bangkok,
a monk contemplates a row of golden eagles called
garudas,* divine symbols of the sky in Hindu mythology.

*A huge Buddha image at Koh Samui is plastered with
bits of gold foil. Worshippers keep adding gilt as a means
of making merit, to be rewarded in a future incarnation.*

King Bhumibol and Queen Sirikit offer food to Buddhist monks in New Year's rites. Here the Queen salutes a monk with a gracious gesture in making her offering.

Early on New Year's Day, monks form in solemn lines at the royal palace in Bangkok for the annual ceremony of alms-giving by the highest dignitaries of the state.

In an inner pavilion of the
Grand Palace, Queen
Sirikit is photographed
wearing a richly embossed
court dress adapted from a
traditional Thai style.

The King is a man of many talents. Going for a sail
with his son, Prince Vajiralongkorn, he takes the tiller of
a small boat that he built in his own home workshop.

A fine jazz musician who can play several instruments as well as compose, King Bhumibol joins the Crown Prince in a saxophone duet.

In the shadowy interior of a Northern teak forest, lumbermen cross a jungle

stream with their work elephants, and a baby elephant tags along.

*Teak elephants, working in
tandem, hoist a big log into
the air with their tusks.
Loaded onto a flatcar,
the wood will be railroaded
to some nearby waterway.*

*Teak logs which have been
floated downriver from the
North are herded into a klong
near a sawmill in Bangkok,
ridden as they go by a
surefooted Thai lumberman.*

A tin worker at a smelting plant in Phuket, an island just off the coast of Peninsular Thailand, has goggles to protect his eyes from the glare of the blast furnace.

In the smelting plant, a workman guides a crane hook into position, while molten tin fills up a boxlike form at the left. Thailand now refines most of its own tin ore.

Like a scene in some classic Oriental painting, fishermen at evening are

silhouetted against a setting sun on the Gulf of Thailand.

In a corner of his shop, a stonecutter chips away at his
trade in the town of Ang Sila, near the Gulf of
Thailand. His possessions on display include a caged bird.

Newly-painted parasols are put out to dry in the village
of Borsarng, where parasol making is a cottage
industry traditionally occupying the entire population.

At one of the country's air bases, a young fighter pilot equipped with oxygen mask gets ready to take off in a jet trainer of the Royal Thai Air Force.

The Friendship Highway, a road built with American aid and U.S. earth-moving equipment, cuts straight as a ruler across the flatlands of Central Thailand.

Down below the road embankment, a girl tends a water buffalo. The powerful animal has served for centuries as a natural farm tractor throughout all of Southeast Asia.

Thai boxing is a rugged sport in which opponents use their feet as well as their hands. Here a mighty kick is being blocked during a match in a Bangkok stadium.

*At a beauty contest in Chiengmai, the smiling
contestants, each shielded from the sun by a bright
parasol, are driven through town in a parade of open jeeps.*

*Proud in her gown of pure Thai silk, wearing the
diadem which is the badge of the contest winner, and
bedecked with flowers, Miss Chiengmai poses for a picture.*

On a stream in Southern Thailand, a traditional race between rival teams of

paddlers draws a happy crowd to the river bank on a local festival day.

In an outdoor painting class, students at the University
of Fine Arts in Bangkok work at their easels by the
edge of a tree-lined canal that was once a city boundary.

*Experimenting in one of the science laboratories of
Bangkok's Chulalongkorn University, an earnest student
watches the reaction of chemicals in a test tube.*

At a temple school in the village of Bangpakong, three
and four-year-old children learn both the Thai and
Roman alphabets under the direction of a youthful monk.

During recess, girls join hands in a circle for a game on
the temple grounds. Although conducted in religious
surroundings, schools such as this are run by the state.

Children recite the day's lesson in a village school.
For this boy and girl, as for most of their contemporaries
growing up in Thailand today, the future looks bright.

City Plaza and Village Square

MID-APRIL in Thailand is the peak of the dry season. It is a time when men, plants, and the earth itself thirst for the cooling rain. The weather is the sort that generates melancholy and riots in other places. In Thailand it sets loose a midsummer madness called Songkran. In the Northern city of Chiengmai — in the region of teak forests, orchids and beautiful women — tens of thousands of young and not-so-young Thais take to the streets to throw water at one another in a three-day open season of festival and fun.

Her soaked blouse and slacks clinging to her, a young woman giggles and squirts an atomizer in the face of every male who crosses her path. Not far away, two young men in loud sport shirts are drenching another girl. A traffic

138

policeman at the crossroads grins sheepishly as two women in shocking-pink *pasins* (sarongs) and *pasabais* (blouses) empty their silver bowls of water down his neck. A group of teen-agers stop splashing each other when a monk approaches; then each sprinkles a few drops on the monk's yellow robe reverently, saying: "Sawadee pimai!" (Happy New Year!) In the shallow Ping River, grown-ups and children stand knee-deep in the river bed, dripping wet, and hurl water at everyone in sight, as the zany battle goes on from sun-up to sun-down.

Songkran is a religious festival of "bathing the Buddha," observed from India to China. It also marks the lunar New Year for the Thais, who turn the occasion into a combination of devotional gesture, rain-making ritual, mating game, and pure, effervescent dedication to *sanouk* — which translates roughly as the joy of living. Nowhere else in Thailand is Songkran quite so uninhibited as in Chiengmai, where the festival draws tens of thousands of celebrants. They come in planes, trains, chartered buses, bullock carts and canal boats, from all over the country and from neighboring Laos as well.

The festival starts soberly enough when young and old, wearing many-hued traditional clothes, carry rice, fruits, candies and flowers to the *wats*. There they sprinkle lustral water on the Buddha and on the abbot in a ceremonial bath. At home the young also "bathe" the elders as a sign of respect. From then on, the spirit of *sanouk* takes over. The picturesque and normally placid Chiengmai comes alive with excitement as clusters of gay blades and laughing young women fill the streets, friends and strangers alike taunting one another with watery greetings. Farm girls wearing jasmine flowers in their hair position themselves along the main thoroughfare near the river to sell silver bowls, water squirters, and water from huge oil drums.

A parade snakes out of the great monastery, Wat Phra

Sihing, headed by musicians in medieval costume playing Java pipes, cymbals, gongs, and 12-foot, cannon-shaped drums. Each village of the surrounding area is represented by a group of elders in the coarse blue, pajama-style suits worn in the north country, and a group of village maidens wearing blouses of Thai silk, *pasins* of Chiengmai cotton, and tiny orchids. They carry the silver plates which were piled earlier with offerings, or silver bowls from which sand has been emptied on the temple grounds. In one section of the parade several young men do the spirited folk dance called the *ramwong,* thumping on finger timpani as they step. At another point a team of slender girls in wine-red costume dance the dreamy *fawn lep,* waving the long, curving, brass tips on their fingernails and moving their bare feet in time to the languorous rhythm of cymbals and gongs. Two skinny men dressed as a policeman and an old woman move down the street in a comical jig. They are followed by a giant float representing billowing clouds on which sit seven Songkran Maidens.

Participants in the parade are not immune from watery assault by other revelers in the streets; attractive females, in particular, are sure to be given attention by the young men. But for all the flirtation involved, the merrymakers are careful not to touch one another. Exuberant but not rowdy, coquettish but never orgiastic, Songkran epitomizes the Thai brand of frolic.

Songkran is but one of many joyful traditional events that dot the calendar in Thailand, alternating with the periods of greatest activity on the farms. Each year this festival is followed by a wave of betrothals and weddings. Young people of the villages have several weeks for singing, dancing and courting — until the monsoon rains arrive about the first of June.

With the rains comes the planting season, heralded by

140

the ritual of the First Plowing and the very sacred rites of Visakha Buja, which precedes the Buddhist Lent. Now all the men and women of a village join together in a communal effort, helping each family in turn with the job of sowing the rice and later transplanting the rice seedlings.

After the transplantation and before the harvest comes another period of relaxation. In late October there is a burst of post-Lenten festivals, including Tod Kathin, when it is customary for villagers to present new robes to the monks at the local *wats*. In Bangkok, great crowds turn out to witness the Royal Barge Procession. At this colorful pageant, gilded, 100-foot-long boats like ancient Mediterranean galleys, with soaring prows carved in the likenesses of sacred swans and serpents, glide majestically along the Chao Phraya River, each rowed by 60 scarlet-robed boatmen. One barge carries the King on a raised and canopied throne.

Full moon in November brings the festival of Loy Krathong, in celebration of which people set afloat in rivers and canals little cups made of banana leaves and carrying lighted candles. By this time of year the floods have receded, but the waterways are full. The night air is crisp and invigorating. Under a full moon, the pale landscape becomes dotted with thousands of flickering lights as the little candle-boats drift downstream and finally disappear.

Right after Loy Krathong comes the harvest. The fields are drained of water, and a harvesting schedule is set up in each village for all hands to descend in unison upon the acreage of one household after another. The workers cut the ripened rice stalks with sickles, spread the grains for drying, and then thresh and winnow the rice — each step being preceded by an offering to the particular spirit involved. Harvest brings money to the villagers, and much of it will be splurged at the annual winter fair in the local *wat*.

The typical family in a Thai village lives in a house on stilts, a type of construction that lifts the floor above flood waters, while facilitating air circulation and creating a shaded outdoor area to accommodate farm animals. The house is built of bamboo or teak, and usually has a steep, thatched roof and a spacious front verandah. The house is situated on an acre or less of land near the growing fields. Slender coconut and areca palms, banana plants, papaya trees, clumps of bamboo and flowering shrubs fill the yard around the house. On the grounds are a vegetable garden, a spirit house, a threshing area and a small, thatched granary on stilts, its single door guarded with a dried palm leaf, which serves effectively as a burglar alarm. If the house is away from the water, it has a fenced-in bathing area; a national characteristic of the Thais is a passion for frequent baths. Cats, dogs, chickens and pigs dodge among scampering children in the yard and beneath the house.

The day's routine starts at sunrise, when the housewife gets up to begin her cooking on a clay stove. The monks from the local *wat* come down the road with their alms bowls, and she goes out to offer them food. Meanwhile, other members of the family rise to feed the animals and to get their farming or fishing equipment ready for the day. Then the whole family sits in a circle on the verandah floor for breakfast. Afterwards the young children walk to school; mother, father and older children go to the fields, canals or markets to work; and the old folks stay home to prepare meals and to care for the babies. Except in the busiest season, everybody takes a siesta during the sultry early afternoon. The family gathers again in the evening after work, for dinner, and later they talk around a flickering kerosene lamp, or perhaps drop in to see the neighbors. Usually by 9 o'clock rural Thailand is asleep.

Farming in Thailand is the same back-breaking labor as in other parts of the world — and must be endured in a climate much hotter than most. But the Thai farmer knows how to spice his hard work with *sanouk* even at harvest time. When the neighborhood helpers have finished the day's toil, they usually stay on at the host farmer's place for dinner. There beside a bonfire the elderly chat and sip rice wine while the young people sing and dance. The *pleng keokao,* or harvest song, is sung by teams of opposite sexes. A quick-tongued soloist of one team steps forward to toss a friendly taunt, extemporaneously rhymed, at a member of the other team. Then it is the latter's turn to parry with an impromptu verse. Each sally is chorused in refrain by the soloist's own team, to the accompaniment of rhythmic hand-clapping, hoots and giggles. Many a village belle and hamlet hero have caught each other's heart in this kind of skylarking by the fireside.

The slack season that follows the harvest is a time of special merriment in the villages. Between festivals there are numerous excuses for parties. And between parties one can always journey to a nearby town for a food fest, a *likay* show or a movie. Picnics in the woods are a popular family diversion. Then there are games of many sorts — nearly all of them heavily bet on by the Thais, who are instinctive gamblers.

Upcountry cockfights provide a favorite pastime and an effective method of redistributing rural wealth. A good fighting cock costs up to $250, and elicits as much pride and affection in its owner as a Kentucky thoroughbred. Heroes of another species are the redoubtable Siamese fighting fish—tiny, colorful, and perennially bad-tempered. A mean male, when put into the same bowl with a rival, can tear him into piscatorial ribbons in seconds. The South is the region for bullfighting. Unlike the Spaniards, who enter the bull ring at risk of getting gored, the Thais pit one bull against another and stay comfortably outside the arena to bet on the outcome. A game played everywhere in the country is *takraw,* in which a light, woven rattan ball about the size of a baseball is kicked, kneed, butted and shouldered. The trick is to keep it bouncing around without letting it touch the hand or fall to the ground.

But perhaps the best-loved game for Thais of every age is kite-flying. From February to April, a period during which the southwest monsoon blows strong and steady, kites made of bamboo and rice paper flutter all over Thailand — aerial performers in the shapes and colors of butterflies, fish, hawks, peacocks, centipedes and serpents, ranging in size from five-inch pipsqueaks to 25-foot giants. The most popular thing to do with a kite is to fight another kite. The aerial battle of the sexes — between the huge, star-shaped *chula,* or male kite, and the tiny, diamond-shaped *pakpao,* or female kite — is no child's play in Thailand, but a big-league sport in which there are established teams, umpires, official rules and a national championship. In a kite fight, the wily *pakpao* darts about temptingly over its home territory. The much larger *chula,* flown by a team of up to 20 men, invades the female kite's air space and tries to seize the *pakpao* with its bamboo talons. This is not an easy thing to do. Possessing all the attributes of a *femme fatale* when in the hands of the right team, the *pakpao* can often loop its line around the *chula's* head, thereby causing the *chula* to lose its aerodynamic stability and tumble ingloriously to the ground.

The languid sound of thudding drums and pinging cymbals bespeaks romance for the Thai youth. But quicken the rhythm and add the shrill screech of a Java pipe, and it puts adrenaline into his blood. This is the music to fight by, and it is played by a frenetic three-piece ensemble at every Thai boxing match.

The art of fighting with the feet, together with sword-fighting, was almost a prerequisite for survival in medieval Siam, where the flow of blood stopped only when the rains came. Today the combat is ceremonial and ordinarily nonlethal. Thai boxers, who range from flyweight to light-weight, wear boxing gloves and trunks, like Western pugilists, but here the similarity ends. Their equipment includes a charm cord around the biceps and a sacred head-band, the latter being worn during the preliminaries to a match but removed before the fisticuffs start. The boxers always fight with bare feet.

Every bout starts with a solemn pre-fight ritual. To the ululation of the Java pipe and the gentle beat of drums and cymbals, each boxer kneels in the ring and faces in sequence the direction of his birthplace and the four major points of the compass. He pays obeisance to the guardian spirit of the ring and to his teachers, including those progenitors of the boxing art who died generations ago. Then comes the terpsichorean part of the ceremony, which looks like a cross between a prayer and an underwater ballet. The boxer crouches on his knees, swaying his head and torso and weaving his arms and fists in stylized gestic-ulation to the eerie music. Each man has his own chore-ography, mixing regional movements and those of his own invention with standard movements recognized by fight fans as the Elephant Stomp, the Making of Garlands, or the Four-Faced Buddha. He also includes gestures intended to "hex" his opponent. Usually he moves his hand along the top rope all around the ring to seal off the fighting area from assorted untoward influences such as partial ref-erees, hexing spectators and malicious, wandering spirits.

When both boxers have gone through this deadly seri-ous preliminary, they are at each other. Thai boxing rules are enough to make the Marquis of Queensberry somer-sault in his grave; they allow not only kicking with the feet, but also hitting below the belt and an unrestricted use of elbows and knees. What the contestants lack in solid punching power they make up for in agility. A Thai boxer can jump several feet into the air and slam his knee against his opponent's thigh, ribs, chin or solar plexus. His most dreaded weapon is his unshod foot, which he swings in a wide arc like a heavy whip, with lightning speed — usually at the other man's ear. The perpetrator of such a kick, however, is momentarily vulnerable; an alert adversary can cushion the kick with his elbow or shoulder and administer a counter-kick at the single supporting leg of the attacker, landing him on the canvas in a heap. As the pace of battle quickens, the musicians go into a frenzy, and blood begins to heat all around the arena. Excited fans shout "Sok! Sok!" for more elbow-ramming, and "Kow! Kow!" for more knee action. A knockout, when it comes, is usually administered by a kick.

A universal sport in Thailand — as in many other countries of the world — is gambling on the national lottery. The results of the draw reach the most remote "boondocks" with amazing promptness each week; indeed, weekly provincial newspapers arrange to publish on the day when winning numbers can be announced.

Except for Bangkok, life in the cities of Thailand is still unhurried. Chiengmai, which is the second largest metropolis in the nation, has a population of only 60,000 and a decidedly pastoral tempo. With its medieval city walls and algae-choked moats, Chiengmai is a romantic and relatively unspoiled relic of a bygone era. As such, it has become a haven for fugitives from the bustling capital, including a number of resident Europeans. The lesser cities of Thailand have more the character of contemporary provincial towns, with marketplaces for the sale of local produce, movie houses, and shops which are very largely operated by merchants of Chinese origin.

The neon-lit fantasy of all Thai country people is a visit to Bangkok, where they go in large numbers during the slack season on the farms — to visit relatives, to make a pilgrimage to a famous *wat*, or just to be thrilled by the bright lights and the awesome traffic. Some arrive in the

146

capital with visions of making a great fortune, but settle shortly for jobs as unskilled laborers and find living quarters somewhere along the *klongs*, or canals, of the city.

Life on the *klongs* has remained virtually unchanged for several centuries. Peddlers, taxi drivers, waitresses and other representatives of the urban "working class" occupy teak, bamboo or thatched houses along the banks of hundreds of waterways that radiate out from the city. Although many canals on the Bangkok side of the Chao Phraya River have disappeared before the spread of asphalt and concrete in recent years, those on the side of Thonburi, Bangkok's twin city, are there as picturesque as ever.

Each day at dawn the *klongs* burst into life, as countless river craft begin to move in this Oriental Venice. Long strings of barges, loaded high with sacks of rice from the country and towed by huffing tugs, arrive at riverside rice mills. Other barges begin journeys inland with all kinds of goods from abroad. Crude rafts of teak logs lashed together end their long voyages from Northern forests at the lumber mills. And everywhere sampans bob along, bringing in the day's supply of fresh produce from surrounding farms. These shallow, canoe-type vessels are powered by outboard motors, or rowed or poled by their owners. Country women who pilot the sampans sell fruits and vegetables either at large, wholesale city markets, or direct to the people who live along the *klongs*. Each house has a landing platform for boats. The ice cream man, in a tiny sampan, rings a bell to announce his arrival. Other sampans carry the butcher, the coffee salesman, the pot and kettle repair man, the little girl who sells garlics and red chilies, and the old woman with betel-blackened teeth who has a store of cotton prints, buttons, needles and thread. Colorful and exotic to Western eyes, the floating market is viewed daily by tourists who pay for rides in hundreds of motor launches.

Naked, bronze-bodied little boys — most of whom have learned to swim before they learned to walk — pop out of the brown water like impish porpoises at the approach of the tourist launches. They hitchhike by grasping the gunwales, or dive underneath the boats — laughing, shouting and clowning for the tourists.

The Bangkok of the *klongs* is a world apart from metropolitan Bangkok, which teems with Westernized, upper-class Thais, Chinese merchants, resident *farangs*, and international tourists. Arriving in Bangkok at the rate of half a million a year, the tourists are whisked from busy Don Muang Airport 15 miles along a fast, four-lane highway to their destinations in several dozen modern, air-conditioned hotels. An average three- or four-day stay includes visits to the Grand Palace, leading temples and the floating market, and bus-window views of parks, universities, hospitals and government buildings.

In the old shopping area near New Road and in the modern shops that surround the big hotels, one can browse for such souvenirs as carved teak elephants, bronze Buddhas, niello ash trays, stone rubbings of temple friezes, shimmering Thai silk, gem-encrusted Princess rings, lacquerware and dolls, as well as Japanese cameras and Scandinavian crystalware.

Night life in Bangkok ranges from the sedate to the exact opposite. The city has many good restaurants, offering Continental, French, German, Italian, Scandinavian, Swiss, Chinese, Indian, Vietnamese, Japanese and Korean cuisine. The decor of these places includes almost every style imaginable, from Mexican grass shack to Chinese emperor's palace. *Farangs* may get an inkling of the culinary splendor of old Siam at several tourist Thai restaurants, where the patrons sit on the floor amid a profusion of velvet cushions, dainty ceramics, and jasmine blossoms, to be served by waitresses in traditional dress while taking

148

in a floor show of Thai music and dancing.

For late amusement there are cabarets featuring Thai torch singers, Indian magicians, Hong Kong acrobats, Australian comedians, English strippers and American go-go girls. Almost all of these places supply "hostesses" for the companionship of unattached males. The lonely male tourist is also catered to by numerous small bars that offer frugging partners, ear-splitting hi-fi, and occult darkness, and by Turkish baths that advertise piped-in music and complete bar service.

Quite apart from its transient visitors, Bangkok has an international elite of Thai and Western residents, all of them known to one another. They live in servant-cluttered old mansions or modern, Western-style houses, always with a garden, often by a *klong,* and invariably fronting on a quiet *soi,* or lane. Most of these people have addresses on one of the 50-odd *sois* that give off from Sukhumvit Road, comprising an area known as the European District. Daily they leave their homes in European or Japanese compact cars or chauffeured limousines to go to work in the top offices of embassies, airlines and government departments, as well as American, English, Chinese, Japanese and Danish trading firms. They belong to one or more of the exclusive city clubs, which include the Royal Turf Club, the Royal Dusit Golf Club, the Polo Club and the Royal Bangkok Sports Club.

For Bangkok's international set, the city is a gay and cosmopolitan place, the scene of innumerable cocktail parties and buffet dinners in spacious gardens decorated with paper lanterns and tinkling temple bells. For weekends out of town, there are the nearby resorts of Bangsaen, with scenic beaches and vacation cottages; Pattaya, for swimming, water-skiing, sailing, or just luxuriating in a hotel that could have been transplanted from Waikiki Beach; and Hua Hin, the resort of royalty, which has elegant villas and the finest beach on the Gulf of Thailand.

So much for the city's social elite. A much larger group of Bangkokians belong to a middle class of civil servants, teachers, newspapermen, shopkeepers, secretaries and small businessmen, who live on the upper floors of their business premises or else in modest quasi-modern or traditional teak houses, often with a small garden. They commute to their jobs by bus and taxicab, and lunch on Thai noodles, Chinese fried rice and sandwiches in small restaurants scattered all over the city. A favorite haunt for government employees and show people is *Sorn Daeng* (Red Arrow), the only sidewalk cafe in Bangkok and one of the few authentic Thai restaurants. On its terrace by the Constitution Monument one can sample fiery food and cold beer while watching sinuous girls go by. Most small businessmen work in Sampeng, Bangkok's Chinatown, whose streets and alleys are lined with shops and commercial houses of every description.

The average Bangkokian has many inexpensive amusements. Besides movies and Thai-style cabarets, there is a year-round bazaar on weekends at Pramane Ground, the city's public square. A pleasant thing for a man to do on a holiday is to dine with his family at one of the lakeside restaurants in Lumpini Park, or take them to beautiful Dusit Park to ride a tame elephant or drift in a rowboat in the free-form lake.

Despite an obvious difference in pace, life in Bangkok is similar in many respects to life in the villages of Thailand. As elsewhere in the Orient, the family is a strongly-knit social unit and there is much affection among close relatives. Married children customarily live in a house near that of the wife's parents, thus combining family togetherness with some degree of privacy.

There was a time when Thais did not have family names; a man knew all his neighbors, and called them all by the given names of childhood. But a 1916 law required everybody to have a surname, for legal and official use. Many families chose long Sanskrit surnames that are hard to pronounce and even harder to remember. It doesn't make much difference to the average Thai, who is still addressed for the most part by his first name only. A person named Sulaksana Patibatsarakich, for example, would be called simply Sulaksana or Nai (Mr.) Sulaksana; and, since "sana" is a Sanskrit suffix not pronounced in Thai, verbally he is just Sulak. It is not uncommon for a husband to be introduced to his wife at a party by someone who does not know that they share the same last name.

The Thais love to give children nicknames such as Little Pig or Little Mouse, and often one of these names remains stuck to an individual after he grows up. The 1965 Miss Universe, a Thai girl named Apasra Hongsakula, was better known to her countrymen as Pook (The Fat One), a baby name belying her 35-22-35 adult dimensions.

When a child is one or two months old, a tuft of his hair is shaved off in a ceremony intended to assure for him health, wisdom and good luck. At this ritual, Buddhist monks chant while a Brahman priest normally officiates. The Brahman dips first a shaved coconut and then the newly-shaved baby into a large silver bowl full of water; after this, he puts a cat into the baby's crib, takes it out, and finally puts the baby in the crib to stay. During the ceremony, friends and relatives wave lighted candles to invoke blessings on the child, and then all settle down together for a feast.

A baby is fondled and pampered until the age of about two, when he begins to receive family discipline, including training in a proper respect for his elders. Childhood in Thailand is normally happy and carefree. Both boys and girls appear to glide through adolescence with none of the trauma characteristically besetting teen-agers in Western countries.

In the villages, young people have lots of opportunity for courtship, both at work and at play. A young swain can serenade his girl, joke with her, and whisper sweet nothings in her ear, but almost always within sight of her parents or someone else. The only place a young couple is allowed to be unchaperoned for a moment is on the front verandah of the house. The idea of having two youngsters go out on a date together has become accepted in the urban society of Bangkok, but is still a distinct rarity in rural Thailand. It is taboo everywhere for people of opposite sexes, even engaged couples, to hold hands or otherwise touch one another in public. To hold an arm around one's partner while dancing is shocking to country people. Almost everyone in Thailand loves to dance — but separately.

In the old days parents used to choose marriage partners for their children, but this custom is dying out, even in the villages. However, it is usual for parental consent to be obtained by young people planning to wed. Of the three major milestones in the life of a Thai — birth, marriage and death — the ceremonies connected with getting married are the most casual and relaxed. Although monks and astrologers are involved in preliminary arrangements, they do not formally take part in the wedding. The couple kneel together on a low platform set up in the house of the bride, with their heads or hands linked by a sacred thread. Elders pour lustral water on the bride and the groom from small conch shells, and thereafter they are considered man and wife. Feasting, singing and dancing follow throughout the night, and the newlyweds are ushered into the bridal chamber at the astrologically auspicious hour.

A marriage in Thailand can be dissolved by mutual consent. Six centuries ago the first king of Ayudhya decreed: "If a husband and wife have a physical or mental distaste for one another and desire to be divorced, let it be as they wish; for they two have no further blessing on their union, and therefore should not be compelled to live together." This doctrine has been part of the Thai legal code ever since.

Thai women have always had more freedom than women in most other parts of Asia, and today they enjoy equal rights with men. A suggestion that the fair sex in Thailand may have achieved somewhat more than equality is seen in the fact that some 90 percent of Bangkok's real estate is owned by women. Although often shy and delicate in appearance, the Thai female is usually found to be practical and resourceful — as well as a gay and sometimes mischievous companion.

The Thais love highly spiced food. Their favorite condiments are garlic, chili, an amber-colored fish sauce called *nam pla,* which lends excitement to even the blandest of dishes, and another sauce made of dried, salted shrimps, pounded with sugar, garlic and lime juice. There are about 25 varieties of Thai curries — sweet, sour, bitter and peppery, all pounded at home by the housewife from a dozen or more fresh ingredients. Many regions have specialty dishes, such as the *haem* of the North, a spicy pork sausage, and the *pla daek* of the Northeast, an appetizer made of raw, fermented fish. The list of Thai delicacies, besides shark's fin and bird's nest soup, as in China, includes banana flowers, dried beetles, and red ants' eggs.

A traditional Thai meal begins with an individual plate of rice, surrounded by small dishes of meat, fish and vegetables, a clear soup and a finger bowl. In years past the meal was always eaten with the fingers, but today forks and spoons are in general use. Unlike the pungent main dishes, Thai desserts are extremely delicate — characteristically light, faintly sweet and subtly fragrant. One of the most delicious is made of unripe, green heads of rice, boiled in lightly scented water, pressed through a sieve, and flavored with sugar and thick coconut milk. Another delectable dessert is sago, or tapioca, cooked to just the right consistency with sugar and coconut milk, in a wrapping of banana leaves.

Usually meals are served on the floor or on low tables, and the family diners sit on the floor, where they also sleep — although this custom is changing in the cities. On entering most private homes, and all temples, the Thais leave their shoes outside. To keep one's shoes on inside a house is something like keeping one's hat on in the West.

The universal word of salutation in Thailand is "Sawadee," similar to the Hawaiian "Aloha." Traditionally the Thais greet each other with the *wai,* which is the gesture of putting the palms together as if in prayer. It is a non-religious salutation as common as the Western handshake. But it is far more complicated than a handshake. One *wai* is differentiated from another by the curve and speed of the hand movement, the level at which the palms meet, and the length of time they stay together. Combined with the *krap,* which is the genuflection appropriate for saluting elders, monks and other people of high station, the greeting may be performed in dozens of different ways to fit the occasion of the moment, as well as the exact status that exists between greeter and greeted. The most reverent salutation, seldom seen today, consists of kneeling before a person while *wai-ing* three times, putting the hands on the floor next to the knees after each *wai.* A simplified version is now used to salute members of the monkhood or royalty.

A social taboo frequently violated unknowingly by Westerners in Thailand is to pat someone on the head. The Thais consider the head the most sacred part of the body, the place where the personal spirit resides, and an elaborate etiquette has grown up around this belief. It is considered discourteous to peer over another's head. A person moving past an elder or one of high rank must do so with his or her head on a lower level than that of the other. If the ranking individual is sitting in a chair, one has to walk like a hunchback to pass by; if he is sitting on the floor, the only way to proceed is in a crawl. This behavior puzzles and sometimes infuriates Westerners, who tend to regard it as a feudalistic anachronism. But to the Thais the whole thing is no more strange than the Western male's custom of offering his seat to a woman or walking on the street side of her when passing along a sidewalk.

The feet, opposite to the head, are considered the lowliest part of the body. For this reason, the Thais are careful never to point at another with a foot. Crossing one's legs while conversing with a person is also considered rude; properly, when sitting, the feet should be placed squarely on the ground.

As in the rest of Asia, etiquette in Thailand stresses first and foremost a respect for elders in the society. As a result, growing old is ordinarily less burdensome than in the West; indeed, old age may be looked forward to as a period of great serenity in the closing years of one's life.

Funeral rites in Thailand are far more elaborate than those of birth and marriage. Burial is always by cremation, usually in the local *wat*. Before a body is cremated, monks chant verses from the Buddhist scriptures in a ceremony which is attended by relatives and friends as a last act of making merit for the deceased. At funerals an orchestra plays all day long. After the religious rites, the mourners gather to play chess, feast, and indulge in other cheerful occupations to banish the sorrow of the occasion — characteristic, one might say, of the Thais, who know how to mix *sanouk* even with death.

CHAPTER 6

The Rush to Development

THE LANDSCAPE of Thailand is changing. The vast, emerald-green rice plains, once linked together only by quiet canals and winding elephant tracks, are now crisscrossed by a growing network of highways. The horizon once dominated entirely by *chedi* spires is now dotted with television antennas, radio towers and microwave relay stations. What used to be an insular, little-known kingdom, remote from the rest of the world, finds itself overrun with tourists, businessmen, military men, international agency representatives, correspondents, and Western expatriates of a new breed. Many of these people have brought in new ideas and new technologies, helping to generate massive new wealth in the country. Today Thailand has one of the most stable of all international currencies, and in recent years the country has enjoyed a rate of economic growth un-equaled elsewhere in Southeast Asia. The individual Thai's income has risen 44 percent in a decade.

Thailand today, as for many years in the past, is an important exporter of rice, rubber, tin and teak. Its economy is heavily dominated by rice, to the cultivation of which both the land and the Thai temperament seem particularly suited. Thailand annually ships abroad more rice than any other nation. Next in importance in world trade is Thai rubber, which became a major export during World War I, enjoyed a post-World War II boom, but then began to suffer severe competition from synthetic rubber. Unlike the situation in Malaya, natural rubber plantations in Thailand are small and many of the trees are under age; therefore Thai rubber is not of the best quality available on the international market.

Tin has been a big money-earner for Thailand through most of its history, and the country's estimated 1,000,000-ton reserves of this metal should keep Thai miners busy for another hundred years. Tin deposits on the Peninsula were first exploited by Chinese settlers in the 15th Century. The original, ant-like assault by hundreds of coolies individually digging out and carting away the ore in baskets has now been largely replaced by modern methods of extraction. On Phuket Island, off the west coast of the Peninsula, towering bamboo structures resembling ski runs stand above huge open pits. In these man-made canyons of sand and gravel—yellow-ochre in color—the miners use high-pressure streams of water, like firemen with hoses, to break off chunks of loosened earth containing the tin ore. Muddy riverlets are formed, flowing toward the lowest level of the pit, which becomes an artificial lake. Here the mud soup is sucked up by a powerful pump and drawn to the top of the bamboo structure, where it is dumped, to cascade down a long, inclined sluiceway. While sand, clay and earth are swept all the way down by the flow, heavier particles of tin ore settle behind tiny cleats on the sluiceway floor, to be collected periodically.

Some of the richest tin deposits are located offshore. Here the extraction is done with floating dredges that bite into the bottom of shallow bays and inlets, lift the silt aboard and wash it, in a continuous process. (The world's first tin dredge was designed by an Australian prospector at the beginning of this century, after he had watched Chinese miners digging tin ore from the bottom of Phuket Harbor by building dykes and bailing.)

The ore from Thai tin mines used to be sent almost entirely to Malaysia and Europe for processing. But in 1963 a modern smelting plant, owned jointly by America's Union Carbide Corporation and Thai investors, was completed at Phuket. This plant, standing just back of the palm-fringed, white coral beach, by the cobalt-blue sea, is very likely the world's most scenically situated tin smelter. Since its erection, the Phuket plant has greatly increased the number of its furnaces to handle the spectacularly increasing volume of tin ore being extracted. Thai ore is of the highest grade, and the search for it in the 1960s brought on something very much like the 19th Century California gold rush. In one four-day period, no fewer than 350 applications for tin exploration permits were received by the authorities in Bangkok. Thailand became the world's second largest producer of tin in 1966 (next after Malaysia).

Teak is one of Thailand's greatest economic assets, because it is hard, durable, even-grained, and so resistant to termites, fire and weathering that it survives for centuries in the tropics. For generations this wood has been logged for domestic and export use — to make furniture, floors, wood paneling and the decks of ships. Teak trees in the Northern valleys are not cut until they reach a diameter of two feet, which means an age of about 150 years. A tree selected for cutting is first "girdled" with an axe — a deep ring being incised around the lower trunk to kill the tree, which is then left standing for two years to dry out. This procedure is dictated by the fact that fresh teak contains too much water to float. At the end of two years' time, trained elephants fell the trees with their powerful trunks — normally during the rainy season, when the timber does not splinter easily and the elephants work best. The felled trees are trimmed of small branches and cut into logs. These are dragged by elephants to nearby waterways or to a place where they can be loaded onto narrow-gauge railroad cars for longer trips to the water.

Throughout the rainy season, loggers and elephants are busy tumbling the logs into mountain rivers and streams, which all flow southward toward Bangkok. Along river rapids and in narrow stretches are watch stations where men and elephants stand by to ease expected logjams. Sometimes it is necessary to build a temporary dam across a shallow stream to back up the water above a logjam; when the water builds up enough pressure to burst through the dam it creates a sudden flood, sending the logs off down-river.

At strategic assembly points downstream the individual logs are lashed together into rafts, which vary in shape, size and rigidity to suit the characteristics of different waterways. Made up of 200 to 400 logs, each raft has rudders fore and aft, a captain's lookout tower, a crew hut, and two sturdy poles trailing behind. These are for thrusting against the river bottom when it is necessary to maneuver the raft. During the long journey downstream, the logs are measured and taxed at several government stations along the way. The entire voyage, interrupted by dry seasons when the raft may be stranded for many months, usually takes three or four years' time. On arrival in Bangkok, the rafts are broken apart and the logs are sold, for finishing at riverside lumber mills. (The largest and heaviest teak logs, however, have been known to take as long as 12 years to make the trip.)

Teak production in Thailand reached a peak of 13.7 million cubic feet in 1931, but dropped to less than half this figure by the mid-1960s because of an earlier lack of reforestation. A government conservation program now requires that new trees be planted as fast as the old are being cut.

While not a major item in the national economy, traditional handicrafts are important to the villagers of many areas as a sideline to farming and other occupations. The great increase in tourism in the age of jet air travel has caused a boom in the market for souvenirs, stimulating the production of inexpensive, hand-manufactured products. Some crafts that were recently in serious decline have been revived and made to flourish as a result.

One of the most famous and long-established of Thai handicrafts is the production of lacquerware. This craft received great emphasis during the Ayudhya era, later almost died out, but in recent years has been resuscitated with the aid of improved techniques from Japan. The best Thai lacquerware traditionally comes from the region of Chiengmai. Workers here extract a gray sap from a tree of the sumac family and filter it through a piece of cloth to obtain a resinuous oil. Stored in jars and protected by a layer of water, the oil turns into the jet black, sticky substance which is called lacquer. This natural varnish is used to coat furniture, decorative panels, bowls, dishes, vases, water jars and cigarette boxes. The base material of lacquerware may be woven split-bamboo, carved teak, papier-mache or earthenware. At least three layers of lacquer are applied over the base with a bamboo brush. After each coating the pieces are left to dry in cool, dark huts, and then polished with powdered stone, rice husk ashes and coarse leaves. The final layer is polished with water and powdered fired clay, leaving the surface with a glistening shine.

Lacquerware is usually decorated with engraved or painted designs, which are gilded or — in the old days — inlaid with mother of pearl. The most popular designs now used are traditional Thai patterns. A drawing is first traced on the lacquered object, and all parts that are to remain black are covered with a gummy yellow substance which will dissolve in water. A thin layer of lacquer is then applied over the whole surface, and before this is completely dry the area of the pattern is covered with gold foil. After 24 hours the object is washed in water. The yellow gum and the gold adhering to it disappear, and the gold design is left in the un-gummed areas.

Many villages of Thailand specialize in a single craft, often with each household of the village devoting attention to only one detail of that craft. In the parasol village near Chiengmai, for example, people in some homes split and shape bamboo; others assemble the bamboo strips into parasol skeletons; still others fasten on the paper covering, waterproof the parasols with resin oil, and paint on floral designs. There are villages spinning, weaving and dyeing silk or cotton, villages producing hand-wrought silver bowls and plates, villages carving teak elephants and salad bowls, villages weaving baskets, making pottery, and fashioning pewterware, bronze Buddhas and temple bells. Handicrafts are practiced by city-dwellers, too; along the *klongs* of Bangkok, skilled workers turn out kites, spirit houses, dolls, bronze cutlery, and handsome nielloware — the last-named being silver and bronze spoons, ashtrays, bracelets and brooches that are inlaid with colored alloys.

Thailand before World War II had a modest position in world trade, but an economy that provided reasonable living standards and national stability. Then Japanese troops landed in Thailand at the time of Pearl Harbor and

161

forced the nation into the Axis camp. During the war the occupation forces extracted huge levies of rice to feed Japanese soldiers, and pillaged the Thai treasury of money equivalent to 15 years of Thailand's normal budgetary expenditure. On V-J Day Thailand found itself in a painful situation. Its currency — the baht, or tical — which had been pegged during the occupation to the Japanese yen, was almost worthless. The government's reserve of gold and "hard" currency to back up its outstanding notes had dropped to less than 17 percent. Worst of all, since technically it was a defeated "enemy," Thailand was required by Britain to pay reparations amounting to 1.5 million tons of rice.

But the bad times would soon be over. In late 1946 Britain reduced its reparations demands to no more than a token sum. And in 1950 the United States — which had all along considered Thailand an occupied country rather than an enemy — gave Thailand its first direct government aid of $10 million. These and other developments brought about a swift economic recovery in the nation. Having luckily escaped any physical devastation in World War II, Thailand now began to feed the rest of war-damaged Asia with its surplus rice.

A major factor in the economic about-face occurring at this time was a system of multiple exchange rates instituted by the Thai government in 1947. Under the law, rice exporters were required to transfer their foreign exchange earnings to the government in exchange for baht at the official rate. This measure enabled Thailand to build up an exchange equalization fund with which the government has stabilized the baht ever since by buying or selling gold and foreign currencies whenever needed on the world market. By 1951 currency reserves reached 100 percent, and subsequently rose even higher. The baht had earned the reputation of being one of the world's soundest varieties of money.

162

The postwar recovery of the 1950s was turned into a boom in the 1960s when the Thai government began to develop the country's economic potential systematically. Impetus was provided by a World Bank mission which visited Thailand in 1958 and afterwards published a report on the Thai economy advocating a strong program of economic planning. The recommendations were heartily agreed to by the Thai government, which promulgated a $1,600-million Six Year National Development Plan for 1961-1966, and followed this with a $2,500-million Five Year Plan for 1967-1971.

The two plans embody a combination of government programming and old-fashioned *laissez faire,* aimed at raising the national standard of living while at the same time promoting a sustained industrial growth. Planning is concentrated at first on the building of what economists call a nation's infrastructure. This is the basic structure for economic growth, including facilities for transportation, communication, irrigation, electrical power, and agricultural research and experimentation. During the latter stages of a plan, increasing emphasis is given to facilities for community welfare, such as housing, education and social insurance.

Most infrastructure development projects in Thailand involve some degree of international financial and technical aid. While many nations have participated, the bulk of the outside financing has come from the United States and from the U.N.-sponsored World Bank. The amount of government-to-government aid is often less important than its catalytic value in getting a development program started. A 1966 report by an evaluation team of the United Nations Economic and Social Council pointed out that the total of all forms of economic aid from all international and bilateral sources constituted at that time only a fraction of one percent of Thailand's over-all economic effort. "By any form of analysis," reads the report, "the conclusion must be that the activities of the Thai people have been the basis of their own prosperity over the past 15 years."

Coordinated with development planning is the creation of an investment climate which is to private enterprise as Thailand's natural climate is to tropical vegetation. The Thai government began to encourage new private investment in the economy as early as 1954, when the first investment law was enacted. But little headway was made at first because the encouragement given was spotty, and because the government itself had been going into commercial undertakings, thereby providing stiff competition to individual capitalists. This practice was a holdover from the days of government monopolies in old Siam; paradoxically, it coincided with the economic tendencies of many newly independent nations in Asia that were being swept by tides of nationalist feeling after World War II. By the 1960s, however, Thailand was definitely moving away from the philosophy of government-in-business. After several revisions, a Promotion of Industrial Investment Act was promulgated in 1962, establishing Thailand as one of the most attractive countries of the world for the transactions of international investors and financiers.

The government still has monopolies in public utilities, railroads, domestic airlines, communications, tobacco processing, and the manufacture of playing cards. It still owns and operates plants for making cement, paper, leather goods, and such minor items as shoe polish and paper clips. The national policy, however, has been to curtail the existing government-owned industries while encouraging new private investment by both Thai citizens and foreigners — mainly in manufacturing, but also in mining, fishing, agricultural processing and tourism.

Private enterprises on the "promoted list" are given a variety of inducements, including freedom from import duty on machinery and other capital equipment and a five-year holiday on duties for raw materials, a business tax exemption on exported products, and a five-year forgiveness of income tax beginning with the first year of profits. Furthermore, the promoted enterprises are allowed to own land, to import technicians and skilled workers outside of regular immigration quotas, and to remit abroad their profits and loans received in foreign currencies. Their products are protected by tariffs on similar items imported from abroad. They are guaranteed against the possibility of nationalization and against damaging competition from government-owned industries.

Foreign capital in Thailand today includes American private investment in well over 100 enterprises, among which are companies for manufacturing, oil refining, construction, trading, banking and insurance. Among corporate investors are such big names as Colgate-Palmolive, Eveready, Firestone, General Electric, I.T.T., Merck Sharp & Dohme, Pan American World Airways, Ray-O-Vac, Singer, Unilever, Union Carbide, and Warner-Lambert. Sizeable investments also have been made by the businessmen of Japan, Nationalist China, Britain, Denmark and Australia. Other investors, attracted by a reported average profit of 20 percent annually after taxes, come from the Netherlands, West Germany, France, Switzerland, Iran, India and Malaysia.

Government planning, international investment, and the prosperity resulting from both have profoundly affected Thailand. Most noticeable is the great proliferation of highways, irrigation and hydroelectric projects, port and airport facilities, and modern communications lines.

Ban Klang Yai, a village of 400 in the Northeast, is some 30 miles from the city of Udon and only 10 miles from the Mekong River, across from Vietiane, the capital of Laos. Yet as late as 1965 it was virtually in the middle of nowhere. The village is in an area of good soil that yields rice, tobacco and bananas. But during past rainy seasons the dirt tracks leading into the village turned glutinous, making it impossible even for bullock carts to move. In 1965 a 380-mile, modern, all-weather highway was completed, linking two of the northernmost cities of the Northeast — Nongkai and Udon — to Bangkok. The next year one of the numerous feeder roads built under the Accelerated Rural Development (ARD) program of the Thai government reached to Ban Klang Yai. The impact on this village was dramatic. With the road came a resident midwife sent by the government, and before long there were visits by government experts on agriculture, sanitation, and the prevention of disease. The villagers found that they could diversify their planting and grow such valuable crops as kenaf, now that they had year-round access to the outside market.

The Nongkai-Bangkok Highway is a joint Thai-U.S. project involving U.S. aid and experienced American consulting engineers. Young Thai engineers have received on-the-job training while participating in the construction work at every stage. One segment of this road, a 90-mile stretch between Saraburi and Korat, was christened the Friendship Highway in token of the good will signified by the joint construction effort.

The highway's trunk line has cut driving time between Bangkok and Nongkai from several weeks in the worst season to a single day. Its 500 miles of feeder roads are syphoning produce of many sorts from the vast Northeast hinterland to the nation's major population centers and ports. Everywhere the roads reach, new sales possibilities are created, new crops are introduced, and farm acreage zooms. Not surprisingly, with the expansion of highways has come a doubling in the number of motor vehicles in Thailand.

Coordinated with highway construction is another high-priority program of the Thai government – a national irrigation and hydroelectric power network. In 1964 the first phase of the Yanhee Multi-Purpose Project was completed, supplying electricity to 14 provinces. Soon power rates in the Bangkok area were being reduced, and consumption of power began to increase sharply due to the presence of new industries. By the late 1960s, demand for power in Thailand was growing at a rate of 20 percent annually.

The nucleus of the great Yanhee Project is the Bhumibol Dam across the Ping River, a tributary of the Chao Phraya River near the historic site of Sukhothai. This 500-foot-high dam is the largest in Southeast Asia and the seventh largest in the world. When completed in 1975, its total capacity of 560,000,000 kilowatts will supply 37 provinces with power and will irrigate some 800,000 acres of farmland. Another huge, multi-purpose project is the Sirikit Dam, named in honor of the Queen, which will one day generate 300,000 kilowatts for Northeast Thailand. Dozens of other dams either have been completed or are under construction in different parts of the country – most of them of modest dimension, designed to meet the specific needs of a particular area. In this category is the Kaeng Krachan Dam across the Petchburi River, an area of recurrent drought not far from the resort beach of Hua Hin. The dam was completed in 1966, and had an immediate effect on the people of the surrounding countryside. Mah Phangam, a septuagenarian who had farmed for more than half a century in that locality, expressed the sentiment of his fellow villagers when he remarked: "It used to be that anyone with any ambition who happened to be born around here moved away as soon as he was old enough. Now the dam has changed all that. New people are actually moving here from other places." Thousands of Mah Phangam's countrymen, in all parts of Thailand, are having similar experiences, as new roads and new irrigation projects change the character of the land.

A number of dam projects in Northeast Thailand will eventually be integrated into the colossal Lower Mekong Basin Scheme, the "Asian TVA," which will one day provide electricity, irrigation and flood control to all the nations bordering the lower Mekong River: Cambodia, Laos, Thailand and Vietnam. Participating in this multi-million-dollar scheme, besides the four countries directly affected, are 21 other nations of the world, 11 United Nations agencies, and three international foundations.

Thailand is modernizing the docking facilities of Bangkok, which is a regular port of call for 28 shipping lines. The government is also improving Bangkok's Don Muang Airport to be ready for huge jetliners of the future, while at the same time planning the construction of a second jetport to handle the constantly increasing traffic in this major crossroads of Southeast Asia.

In communications, Thailand is in the forefront of late-20th Century developments. Besides 90 radio stations for disseminating news and entertainment, the country has a chain of coastal weather broadcasting facilities for the benefit of fishermen. Five television stations provide almost every region with live Thai and canned U.S. programs. For internal message-sending, Thailand has a TELEX, or teleprinter system, as well as a microwave system linking several provincial cities to Bangkok. Finally, as a member of the International Telecommunications Satellite Consortium (INTELSAT), Thailand will be integrated into the international, all-weather network of telephone, teletype, facsimile, radio and television signals being relayed the world over by means of satellite.

With all the impact of modern developments in industry and communications, agriculture remains the solid basis of the Thai economy. Improvements are being sought on the farms as elsewhere. Rice is plentiful in Thailand, but during the 1960s the nation's annual increase in rice production failed to keep pace with a three percent annual increase in population. Furthermore, the average yield per acre of rice was considerably less than that obtained in Nationalist China and Japan. New irrigation projects, the increased use of chemical fertilizer, and agronomic research are now changing this situation for the better.

Agricultural diversification is an important objective of both government and private interests in Thailand. Large numbers of farmers in the Northeast — traditionally a depressed area economically — have been made aware that either kenaf or corn gives them a per-acre income nearly 70 percent greater than rice. Today the production of kenaf, corn and cassava, all negligible in the past, has increased to such an extent that these crops are major items in international trade, constituting about a quarter of the total value of Thai exports.

While agricultural production, helped by diversification, has been rising in recent years, it nevertheless represents a declining percentage of the gross national product of Thailand. The economy is shifting, slowly but steadily, away from the predominance of agriculture. Among many industrial operations figuring in this economic shift, perhaps none is more significant as an example of flourishing individual enterprise than the revival of the Thai silk business.

The ancient art of silk weaving was almost moribund in Thailand by the 1940s, because of the increasing availability of cheap, machine-woven fabrics from abroad. The last of the skilled Thai craftsmen were abandoning their hand looms and turning to other trades when a remarkable American entrepreneur named James H. W. Thompson — known to a whole generation of his Bangkok contemporaries as Jim Thompson — stepped in to reverse the course of events. Thompson had been sent to Thailand at the end of World War II as an O.S.S. captain, and subsequently became an official of the U.S. Legation in Bangkok. A man with an eye for beauty, trained as an architect, he found himself fascinated by the iridescent colors and nubbly texture of Thai silk. He bought several pieces without having any idea of what to do with them. Then a friend jokingly remarked that Thompson ought to go into the silk business, and he began thinking seriously about it.

One day Thompson found a piece of silk of particularly exquisite design in pink, emerald green and crimson, and traced the cloth to its weaver, a man who had taken up part-time work as a plumber. At Thompson's request, the plumber joyfully returned to his home loom and wove half a dozen 15-yard lengths for the American. Thompson resigned his government job and headed for New York with the samples. U.S. designers, decorators and fashion editors were impressed with the exotic look of the Thai product, and Thompson returned to Bangkok in 1947 with a number of orders. He had only $700 in initial capital, but he boldly persuaded about 200 ex-weavers to return to their looms, and supplied them with raw silk, fast-color Swiss dyes, and massive doses of Yankee optimism.

Business was slow at first. Thompson used to drape lengths of brilliant cloth over his arm and stroll through the tourist-haunted lobby of the Oriental Hotel. Whenever anyone asked him what he was carrying, he would casually explain that he got the silk from a certain shop owned by a Chinese friend. Thai silk got its big boost when it was used for costumes in Rodgers and Hammerstein's Broadway production of *The King and I,* and received extensive publicity in this connection. Today the Thai Silk Company on Suriwongse Road — better known as "Jim Thompson's place" — ships its bolts of luminous material to more than

170

20 countries. High fashion designers the world over prize this fabric for use in evening gowns and other creations of special elegance. The company keeps weavers busy at some 600 looms in homes and small factories scattered along the *klongs* of Bangkok. Thai friends and associates of Jim Thompson's early days are the majority stockholders of the thriving enterprise. Thompson himself tragically and unaccountably disappeared in 1967, while strolling outdoors during a visit to a friend in Malaya.

Measured by any standard, Thailand's economic progress since World War II has been impressive. During the 1960s the gross national product increased about seven percent annually, a rate among the highest of all countries. Although per capita income is far below that of Western Europe or the United States, living standards are high by Asian comparisons, and the consumption of goods is in a steady rise. Because of the influx of machinery and other capital goods, imports lately have been increasing faster than exports. But this trade gap has been more than made up by capital inflow, including the foreign investments and tourist dollars that have given Thailand a consistently favorable balance of payments.

The economic picture is not entirely rosy. Lacking an extensive industrial base, it is not possible for Thailand to achieve the kind of indefinite rise in living standards contemplated by nations more fortunately endowed; a limit to economic growth eventually will be reached. But much can be accomplished before that day arrives.

The temptation is strong for an economically developing nation, in channeling its limited resources, to plump for a prestige steel mill or a grandiose sports stadium, instead of such prosaic projects as earth-filled dams and agricultural diversification. The Thai government has shown great realism in facing up to the economic facts of its existence. The consequence is described in two recent studies by American government agencies. A U.S. Department of Commerce report on Thailand reads: "The basic health of the economy, the willingness of the government to pursue wise economic policies, and the stable political climate augur for a continuation of the extremely favorable economic outlook." The U.S. Agency for International Development sized up investment prospects like this: "The prosperous economy of Thailand offers attractive opportunities for private investment in many industries. Rising national income and improving standards of living provide a growing market for a wide variety of goods. The country is stable and progressive, and government policies aimed at diversified economic development create an environment favorable to private investor participation."

More than six centuries have passed since King Rama Kamheng of Sukhothai laid down the foundations of free enterprise in Thailand. "Whoever wants to trade in elephants, so trades; whoever wants to trade in horses, so trades..." reads his famous inscription. Some of the commodities now being dealt with in Thailand are new since the days of Rama Kamheng. But the rules of economic life in the country haven't really changed at all.

CHAPTER 7

Holding Together a Nation

FOR TWO HOURS the jeep bucked along dusty roads in the Northern hill country of Thailand. The driver reached a point where wheeled vehicles could go no farther, and he and his passenger climbed out. The driver, a slim, young-looking man with handsome, chiseled features, was Bhumibol Adulyadej, King Rama IX of Thailand, whose full title would be given ceremonially as His Majesty the Supreme Divine Lord, Great Strength of the Land, Incomparable Might, Greatest in the Realm, Lord Rama, Holder of the Kingdom, Chief of the Sovereign People, Sovereign of Siam, Supreme Protector and Monarch.

King Bhumibol's companion on the jeep expedition, a lovely, raven-haired woman with a willowy figure and quick smile, was his royal consort, Queen Sirikit. Both were dressed in rough outdoor clothes, wore heavy-soled sneakers, and carried lunch packs on their backs. For the next five miles they and a group of escorts hiked along rugged mountain trails to reach the remote settlements of hill tribes, to whom they brought medicines and other gifts. These nomadic tribesmen are ethnically not Thai, and live very much to themselves. Nevertheless, because of recent overtures of friendship by the Thai government — symbolized in this case by the King's visit — the hill tribesmen have taken to calling themselves "children of the Thai."

King Bhumibol is a monarch who seriously concerns himself with the problems of his country, and takes an active role in dealing with them. He is no less conscientious about discharging the formal and traditional aspects of his office. Naturally reserved, and given a somewhat solemn look by the glasses he customarily wears, the King performs with great dignity during the innumerable ceremonies of state (often religious observances) at which he is required to officiate. A matter of huge satisfaction to the Thais, who love pageantry of every sort, is the fact that their King looks and acts like a king — in riding the royal barge at the Tod Kathin Festival, in accepting the gift of a sacred white elephant, or in changing at the turning of each season the gilded robes of the legendary Emerald Buddha.

Perhaps even more endearing to his countrymen, a people noted for their enjoyment of life, is the King's obvious propensity for fun. To celebrate a recent wedding anniversary, he and Queen Sirikit invited some 1,000 guests — government officials, foreign diplomats and personal friends — to a Hawaiian-style party at Klaikangwon Palace, on the beach of Hua Hin. Everybody wore bright-colored Hawaiian clothing — the Queen in an Islander's frock with sprays of violet orchids in her hair. A high point of the festivities was the performance of a Hawaiian revue entitled "Dream Island," based on a song of the same name composed by the King and starring the King's eldest daughter, Princess Ubol Ratana. The princess danced the hula barefoot, with several other girls, while her father played the piano as an accompaniment. Later the King moved from the piano to the saxaphone, to the trumpet, the Hawaiian guitar, and back again to the piano.

King Bhumibol is the first king of any nationality ever to have been born in the United States. The event occured on December 5, 1927, in Cambridge, Massachusetts, where the King's father, Prince Mahidol of Songkhla, was studying medicine at Harvard University. Two years later, when Prince Mahidol was serving as a resident physician at a hospital back in Thailand, his medical career was ended by his untimely death. A few years later his widow (she had been a nursing student at Simmons College in Boston) took her daughter and two sons to live in Lausanne, Switzerland. Here Prince Bhumibol attended nursery school and later the Ecole Nouvelle de Chailly — where he studied English, French and German, among other subjects.

When King Prajadhipok abdicated in 1935, Bhumibol's older brother, Ananda, became King at the age of nine, under a regency. But with the exception of a brief visit to Bangkok, the family stayed on in Switzerland through World War II. In 1946, a time of political confusion and uncertainty in Thailand, the Mahidol family returned to Bangkok. King Ananda was now 20 years old. After reigning only a few months, the young king was found shot dead in a palace bedroom, the apparent victim of assassination. The tragedy shocked the entire nation.

In that sad June of 1946 King Bhumibol succeeded to the throne. Soon afterwards he returned to Switzerland to complete his studies at the University of Lausanne. To prepare for his new career at home, he switched from his favorite college subject of science to law. The young King lived with his mother and sister in a modest villa on Lake Leman. During leisure hours he acquired a fondness for photography, *le jazz hot,* sports cars, and the remarkably beautiful daughter of the Thai ambassador to France, Princess Sirikit Kitiyakara, a second cousin. They were engaged in London in 1949, on the occasion of her 17th birthday party.

King Bhumibol returned to Thailand the following year. After officiating at his brother's cremation in March, he got married in April and had his coronation on May 5, 1950.

The King lives today with his family in Bangkok, not in the historic Grand Palace, but in Chitralada Palace, a modern residence which has the character of a comfortable villa. Every morning he breakfasts with the Queen while their younger children are hustled off to a school on the palace grounds. His day is packed with official duties such as the signing of laws, judicial pardons and government appointment lists. Identifying closely with the youth of Thailand, he often hands out diplomas at university commencement exercises. He usually lunches with the Queen, perhaps in company with friends or important guests. He sees the Prime Minister often, and gives audiences to a stream of visitors ranging from foreign heads of state to local school children.

For relaxation the King breeds dairy cattle, raises improved strains of rice, plays badminton, and runs a home workshop in which he has assembled both a sailboat and a working helicopter. Among his other distinctions, Bhumibol is the only king to have had a piece played on Broadway, a song entitled *Blue Night,* which appeared in Mike Todd's *Peep Show* of 1950. His first composition, *Falling Rain,* is a perennial hit in Thailand. Every week a group of amateur musicians who call themselves the Chitralada Orchestra come to the palace to join the King in a jam session. This extraordinary monarch is also an enthusiastic camera buff and an oil painter of some talent.

The royal couple often spend weekends at Hua Hin — swimming, sailing and water skiing with the children: Princess Ubol Ratana, born in 1951, Crown Prince Vajiralongkorn (1952), Princess Sirindhorn (1955) and Princess Chulabhorn (1957). All four have had their earliest schooling in Bangkok. But for his secondary education the Crown Prince was enrolled at an English public school.

Although properly deferential in public to her husband, the King, Queen Sirikit is an extraordinary personality in her own right. Like her husband, she paints, plays the piano, and speaks fluent English and French. A devoted parent, she makes a point of spending part of each day with her children. When the King served his priesthood in 1956 she acted as Regent in his stead, officiating at state ceremonies with characteristic composure. She is active in charity work of many kinds, and serves as president of the Thai Red Cross Society.

Thailand at one time had one of the world's most absolute monarchies. Especially after the conquest of Angkor, in 1433, the Brahmanistic concept of *devaraja,* or the "divine king," was taken up by Thai rulers as it had been in Cambodia. This concept of royal infallibility and illimitable power was softened somewhat by Theravada Buddhism and by the innate gentleness of the Thai character. Nevertheless, the Thai king was considered so sacred that whenever he left the palace all the commoners along his route were required to close their doors and windows lest they commit the unforgiveable crime of looking upon the royal presence. The penalty for touching royalty was death — a taboo that had a highly unexpected result in 1881, when Queen Sunanda's royal barge upset and the Queen, toppled into the Chao Phraya River, was drowned because no one present dared extend a hand to haul her out of the water.

The old-fashioned absolutism of the Thai monarchy was largely done away with in Victorian times by the liberal-minded King Mongkut and his son, King Chulalongkorn. Thus the country was well prepared for the transition to constitutional monarchy which occurred in 1932.

According to the several Thai constitutions formulated since that date, the King is still sacred and his person inviolable. He is the chief of state, head of the armed forces, and defender of the Buddhist faith (and of other, minority faiths in Thailand, as well). Theoretically, he can exercise authority only through the executive, legislative and judiciary branches of the government. In this respect his legal position is analogous to that of European constitutional monarchs. But because of the general mystique surrounding the Thai monarchy, and the special esteem felt for Bhumibol himself, the influence of the King is far greater than that defined by any statute.

This was illustrated at the time of a border dispute between Thailand and Cambodia in 1962, centering over possession of an 800-year-old Hindu temple, Khao Phra Viharn, that each country claimed. Interpreting the cartographic evidence on which it had to base a decision, the International Court of Justice ruled, by a vote of nine to three, that the temple belonged to Cambodia. The decision enraged just about everybody in Thailand. Cabinet ministers, newspaper editorialists, and the public at large set up a clamor to defy the World Court verdict and hold the temple by force. The country was on the brink of war when the Thai government suddenly announced that it would accept the court ruling under protest.

What happened was that King Bhumibol, feeling that Thailand as a member of the United Nations must obey the rules of that organization and abide by a decision of its judicial body even though it considered the judgment unfair, had made his opinion known to then-Prime Minister

Sarit Thanarat, thus causing Thai diplomacy to reverse course. In a short time the issue of the temple was largely forgotten.

Subtly and without fanfare, King Bhumibol acts as a stabilizing factor in Thai politics and foreign relations. He also is a strong force behind the scenes in promoting Thailand's economic progress, educational improvement, and advance toward fully representative government. The King's prestige is so high that neither dissident politicians nor hostile Cambodians nor even the Communists in and out of the country dare to criticize him. A father figure in the tradition of the earliest Thai kings, and a modernist like his grandfather, Chulalongkorn, King Bhumibol does much to propel his nation along new paths of progressivism.

In old Siam, under the absolute monarchy, all positions of influence in the country were held by members of the aristocracy. Due to the former practice of polygamy and the long duration of royal dynasties, it might be expected that Thailand today would be overflowing with aristocrats. This is not the case because of a unique system by which titles are gradually diminished among the hereditary aristocracy. The King's heirs go down one step in rank each generation, so that eventually a royal descendent is a plain *Nai,* or Mister. The highest rank is *Chao Fa,* or Royal Highness, followed by *Phra Ong Chao,* or Highness, and *Mom Chao,* or Serene Highness. Below these ranks, reserved for royalty, are the descending titles of *Mom Rajawong, Mom Luang* and *Nai.* Today Thailand has some 150 nobles of royal rank and a larger number of *M.R.s* and *M.L.s.* (The blue blood of these last can be detected only by the telltale initials on their calling cards.) Some titles are not hereditary, but are conferred by the King as a reward for meritorious service to the state. For similar reason the King can also raise the rank of a titled aristocrat.

Today most Thai aristocrats work for a living and fraternize freely with commoners. Despite the maintenance of an elaborate court etiquette, class feeling is generally absent in social affairs. The civil service is made up largely of commoners; even senior posts in the government are given mainly on the basis of ability. In education, competitive examinations decide the recipients of many scholarships abroad; promising boys of ordinary family, as well as young aristocrats, are sent to study in Europe and the United States. Western-educated officials, a civil service system modeled after that of Britain, and a long history of independence combine to give Thailand a large corps of experienced government administrators — a national asset of great value that her neighbors in Southeast Asia do not enjoy.

Thailand's first constitution, created in 1932, established a parliamentary government with legislative, judicial and executive branches under the King. But after centuries of absolutism, democratic institutions were not to spring full blown into existence by revolutionary mandate. In the next 30 years Thailand had seven different constitutions and 30 cabinets. Changes of government came with bewildering rapidity, often as the result of carefully planned coups d'état. Such political upsets in Thailand have been almost always bloodless, and have represented in many cases simply a shifting coalition of power among the original revolutionists of 1932.

In 1957 a nonviolent coup engineered by Field Marshal Sarit Thanarat brought down the then-existing government, and the constitution then in force was suspended. With the nation endangered by both internal and external Communism, Sarit assumed very wide-ranging authority to take action in the interests of national security. An interim constitution was promulgated in 1959, and a constituent assembly was appointed to act as a legislative body while at the same time drafting a new, permanent constitution. Sarit, however, remained in power until his death in 1963, when the premiership passed to his deputy, Field Marshal Thanom Kittikachorn. Meanwhile, through all the changes, the solidly-established monarchy and career civil service have given a remarkable continuity to Thai public life.

The executive branch of the Thai government consists of the Prime Minister, the Council of Ministers (members of the Prime Minister's cabinet plus their under-secretaries), and the civil and military services. Major government decisions are made collectively by the Council of Ministers. Regular ministries corresponding to the familiar subdivisions of Western governments are Agriculture, Communications, Defense, Economic Affairs, Education, Finance, Foreign Affairs, Industry, Interior, Justice, National Development, and Public Health.

For administrative purposes Thailand is divided into 71 *changwats,* or provinces, each under a provincial governor appointed by the King upon the recommendation of the Minister of the Interior. The provinces are divided into 509 *amphurs,* or districts, administered by district officials who are also appointed by the central government in Bangkok. On the local level, districts are divided into 4,888 *tambons,* or communes, which are in turn divided into 41,537 *bans,* or villages. Each of the villages is led by a village headman, who is locally elected. The village headmen, in turn, elect the headmen for their respective communes.

A major administrative responsibility in every province is education. At one time Thai schools were run entirely by Buddhist monks, and monks still play a large role in primary education at the village level. The great King Chulalongkorn established Thailand's first government-supported school in 1871, and in 1892 set up a state public school system under a national Department of Education, which later became the Ministry of Education.

King Chulalongkorn's son, King Vajiravudh, founded Thailand's first institute of higher learning, Chulalongkorn University, and in 1921 established a four-year compulsory education program for children between seven and 14. With this measure there came into being a large number of lay schools staffed with salaried teachers, although most of these institutions had to be housed in village *wats*. (Many of the state schools are still on temple grounds.) Since 1921, numerous measures have been taken by the government to extend and improve the classroom training given to Thai youth — especially in recent years. Under the Developmental Plan of 1961-1966, compulsory free primary education was expanded from four to seven years, and the system of grading was reorganized. Due to a lack of facilities and teachers, however, the full implementation of this plan was not expected until 1970. Public expenditures for education have been steadily increased in a decade, until they have reached the vicinity of 15 to 18 percent of the national budget, a proportion higher than that normally allocated to defense.

Literacy in Thailand is now above 70 percent, among the highest in Asia. More than 4,000,000 children, representing 92 percent of those in the age group for compulsory education, are in school. (The remaining 8 percent of school-age children are in villages so remote that educational facilities are not yet available.) The standard curriculum of Thai primary schools gives emphasis to mathematics, science and language — meaning the Bangkok, or national, dialect. In government schools in the South, where the ethnic majority is Moslem, special courses in the Moslem religion and Malay language are offered.

Only a small percentage of primary school graduates thus far are able to go on to high schools. Competition at the high school level is intense, as most civil service posts call for a high school diploma, and the Thais generally look upon government service as a highly prestigious occupation. Vocational schools are popular and important. Thailand, being a predominantly agricultural nation, has a well recognized need for learning of a practical sort in agronomy and the use of modern farm equipment. And its budding industries can absorb some 30,000 new skilled workers every year. Various provincial schools offer courses in agriculture, telegraphy, mechanics, aeronautical engineering, nursing, typing, shorthand and other vocational subjects. The Technical Institute of Bangkok is regarded as one of the best training centers of its kind in Asia. For boys who cannot attend a regular trade school, the Thai government provides short-term vocational courses in a number of rural areas. For girls in remote villages, it sends mobile units to tour the country, offering half-yearly instruction in such subjects as homemaking, cooking, dressmaking and hair styling.

For many years Thailand has had five universities: Chulalongkorn University, Thammasat University, the University of Medical Sciences, the University of Agriculture, and the University of Fine Arts — all in Bangkok. Would-be students in the provinces have had to journey to the capital to go to college, an expensive and not always practical thing to do. To help satisfy a surging new demand for higher education everywhere in Thailand, three regional universities have recently been established — in Chiengmai for the North, in Khon Kaen for the Northeast, and in Pattani for the South. Founded by the Thai government, these universities have had assistance in faculty recruiting from private foundations and corporations in the United States and other countries. The new institutes of higher learning, which have modern buildings and spacious campuses, are the forerunners of similar universities to be established in all major provinces.

Education in Thailand is highly centralized under the government. (The Prime Minister takes special responsibility for the universities.) In general, the Ministry of Education decides on curricula, textbooks, examinations and school hours, while the schools themselves are run either by the Ministry or by local authorities. A national competitive examination at the end of each educational cycle is designed to standardize academic achievement levels and make it possible to select the best qualified students for further advancement. Teachers and school administrators are government employees within the civil service apparatus.

In addition to government schools, Thailand has several thousand private schools, ranging from one-room temple schools in villages to large, long-established institutions sponsored by Western missionaries and by the Chinese community. Private schools are encouraged by the government as long as they meet official requirements, including the use of the Thai language as the teaching medium.

On the welfare front, a number of urgent problems are being met by government action — often with the assistance of United Nations agencies and other outside sources of aid. Before World War II, diseases such as malaria, tuberculosis, nutritional and parasitic ailments plagued a sizeable portion of the population of the poorer areas of Thailand. Malaria was the country's number one killer, responsible for an average 40,000 deaths annually. In the early 1950s, a combined Thai-U.N.-U.S. assault on the disease with drugs, DDT and public education dramatically reduced the mortality rate by five sixths within a few years' time, and by the late 1960s malaria had been almost completely eradicated in Thailand.

Control of other diseases has been less spectacular but nevertheless impressive. An awkward medical problem is that nearly half of the country's hospital beds and two thirds of its physicians are concentrated in Bangkok. Consequently, residents in most rural areas must depend on clinics, dispensaries, and mobile health units for occasional medication and treatment of disease. Facilities for health care have been stepped up under the national economic development plans. On top of a slow but steady increase in the number of medical doctors, there has been an acceleration in the training of midwives, nurses and sanitary inspectors.

Two threats to the national health in Thailand — as in other parts of Asia — have been a lack of adequate drinking water and improper diet. The problems are especially acute in the Northeast. The government is now digging wells and building water filtration plants to insure a supply of potable water in many areas. Bad diet among the Thais is less a matter of poverty than of clinging to traditional habits. The Northeasterners, for example, love *pla daek,* an extract of decayed, raw fish, which can be ruinous to human health because of parasitic worms it contains. Despite government teams tramping into the villages armed with worming medicine and posters reading "Please eat cooked food!", the people of the area for the most part simply will not give up their favorite dish. *Pla daek* and a number of other foods containing liver fluke and similar parasites still infect and debilitate a large share of the population of the Northeast. Some villagers, used to the consumption of river water, with its familiar content of bacteria and other living organisms, are not receptive to water from newly-dug wells because "it doesn't taste good." Attitudes such as these take years and sometimes decades to be changed by public education. But headway is being made.

The leaders of Thailand are well aware that political disaffection in rural areas more often than not is a result of frustration at not being able to earn a decent living; that the problem of Communism, where it exists, has economic roots. The best way to stave off Red insurgency, they believe, is to improve the lot of the common man and his family in the remote villages of the country. Therefore, a large share of government programs to combat health hazards, enrich the diet, and improve the quality of life of Thailand's least favored citizens are being undertaken in the Northeast, where Communist infiltration and subversion have proven a persistent problem.

Operating for some years past have been the government's Mobile Development Units, familiarly known as MDU. An official team in a caravan of vehicles arrives in a village, where the members of the team put on lectures and movies telling of the government's concern for the farmers. Various experts then help the villagers to make fences, dig sanitary wells, and build latrines. They supply the farmers with improved seeds, and instruct them in modern planting methods. Sometimes a nearby hydroelectric development will make it possible for an MDU team to assist the villagers in stringing power lines into their community for the first time. When everything possible has been done in the way of assistance, the MDU team members climb into their trucks and move on to the next village.

Perhaps of even greater importance politically than MDU is the government's Accelerated Rural Development (ARD) program, which has concentrated very largely on the building of country roads. Wherever the roads penetrate, the local economy is stimulated and insurgency tends to disappear.

There is nothing hopeless about the situation in Northeast Thailand. This area is not a misery-steeped Bihar, nor even an Appalachia. Year-round rainfall is sufficient, though uneven; many places have good and even lush vegetation. (But there are difficulties to be overcome in irrigation.) The soil is much better than that of the poorer

186

sections of China or the Middle East. The people may suffer from dietetic malnutrition but not from hunger. Their clothes are humble but never ragged. A visitor is impressed with the fact that the Northeasterners feel pride in growing their own food and weaving their own cloth. And they are as charming, witty and fun-loving as the rest of the Thais.

The point has often been made that because the Northeasterners are of Lao origin, their loyalty in a showdown might be with the Communist Pathet Lao rather than with Bangkok. The possibility is strongly doubted by Western anthropologists and others who have studied the situation at close hand. Ethnically, the Lao people are a branch of the Thai race. Historically, the country which is called Laos was part of Thailand until the French sliced it off and merged it with Vietnam and Cambodia to form French Indo-China. Eight million of the Lao people reside in Northeast Thailand today, only one million in Laos.· It is true that the Lao of Northeast Thailand have family ties with the Lao in Laos, just across the Mekong River, and that the Communists have used these ties to facilitate their infiltration of Thailand. But the "togetherness" of the two groups is clannish rather than nationalistic.

Thai leaders believe that if economic prosperity and social betterment can be continued, the Northeast will be politically stabilized and Thailand will keep its unity and territorial integrity. A tradition of independence from outside dictation of any kind, the absence of endemic poverty in the country, and the Thai government's earnest, pragmatic development programming — all augur well for the Thai people to maintain their national identity and freedom through whatever trials may come.

187

CHAPTER 8

A Key Role in Today's World

IN THE past two decades, Thailand has emerged as the most economically prosperous and politically stable country of Southeast Asia. By its internal example, and by its leadership externally in promoting regional cooperation and development, Thailand will unquestionably play a key role in the years immediately ahead, as the nations of this much-troubled section of the world act to resolve their problems and move forward toward greater security and a higher over-all living standard.

Thai foreign policy since World War II has been characterized by determined opposition to the spread of Communism in Asia. Thailand was quick to send troops to join the United Nations forces in Korea in 1950. When the SEATO defense alliance was formed in 1954, Bangkok became its headquarters. In the 1960s, the leaders of Thailand openly threw in their lot with the United States against Red aggression in Vietnam. This was not done without raising some natural apprehensions at home; outright participation in the war, it was feared in some quarters, might result in making Thailand itself another Vietnam.

The threat of Communist insurgency is very real in the Northeast, where revolutionists have steadily infiltrated across the Mekong River from Laos. As early as 1950, Red China founded a "Free Thai" organization to encourage insurrection against the Bangkok government among rural Thais living in outlying, border areas. In 1964, China and North Vietnam announced formation of the "Thailand Independence Movement." When South Vietnam appeared on the point of disintegration in 1965, Chinese Foreign Minister Chen Yi publicly stated: "We hope to have a guerrilla war in Thailand before the year is out." Before that year was out, the first armed clash with the Reds took place in Northeast Thailand. Shortly afterwards came a consolidation of the two insurgency movements inspired by Peking and Hanoi into the "Thai Patriotic Front."

It may be that the Communists will make further inroads. But many factors suggest that Thailand will never become another Vietnam. There are extremely significant differences between the two countries. Unlike Vietnam, Thailand has a highly homogeneous population, with no serious antagonisms between regions or between groups. Land tenure is not a problem here; there are virtually no big landlords, and 80 per cent of all Thai farmers own the fields they till. Religion in Thailand is a cohesive, not a divisive force. The country, rich in resources and unplagued by over-population, is not seething with discontent. Having never undergone colonial subjugation, the Thais have no need to search now for a national identity;

thus rebels in the Northeast cannot unfurl the glamorous banner of independence from "Western imperialism" used so effectively by Ho Chi Minh. Finally, the popular King Bhumibol, who inspires the loyalty of Thais everywhere, is a powerful influence for unity in the nation.

Throughout its history, Thailand has always been afraid of a strong, expansionist China. And the militant ideology radiating from Peking in recent years has done nothing to diminish that fear. It was during the 1950s that all the countries of Southeast Asia became acutely aware of newly-expansionist tendencies on the part of the colossus looming to the north of them. Each reacted in its own way, according to the judgment of its leaders. Some, like Cambodia, gambled on friendship with China and accommodation to the Chinese aims; others, like Burma, tried to remain neutral in the contest between expanding Communism of the Peking variety and opposing forces. Thailand decided on a firm stand against encroachment of any kind. At the same time, it began a crash program of "pacification" by government action to raise living standards in the hitherto-neglected Northeast. Speaking of Thailand's resistance to Communist intrusion, Foreign Minister Thanat Khoman explained to a group of Westerners not long ago that the Thais "have never known foreign domination — be it white, be it red, be it brown. We just want to be ourselves, masters of our own destiny."

While acting to preserve independence at home, the leaders of Thailand have at the same time concerned themselves with the larger area of Southeast Asia as a whole. In an age of super-states, the world realizes increasingly that small nations, to compete effectively in the arenas of economics and diplomacy, must rely on cooperative action. Thailand took the initiative in bringing about formation of the Association of Southeast Asia (ASA), a non-military grouping of Malaysia, the Philippines and Thailand, whose first meeting was held in Bangkok in 1961. For a time afterwards, during Indonesia's confrontation with Malaysia, ASA became moribund. But when Sukarno and his neighborhood belligerency faded from the scene, ASA was reactivated in 1966.

A grouping of the same three countries, with the addition of Indonesia and Singapore, was established in 1967 under the lengthier title, Association of Southeast Asian Nations (ASEAN). This organization, also holding its first meeting in Bangkok, issued a declaration that its purpose was "to accelerate the economic growth, social progress and cultural development in the region through joint endeavor."

A larger and more ambitious regional institution is the nine-nation Asia and Pacific Council (ASPAC), which came into being largely through the efforts of Thailand and South Korea in 1966. Besides these two, the countries joined in ASPAC are Australia, Japan, Malaysia, Nationalist China, New Zealand, the Philippines and South Vietnam. Laos has observer status. ASPAC is moving ahead on programs of economic and cultural cooperation; it has under study such possibilities as a central registry of technicians, a food and fertilizer bank, a customs union, and ultimately a common market.

In addition to the efforts of these associations to promote regional advance are important projects of multinational benefit sponsored by United Nations agencies. These projects include the Great Asian Highway, a 35,000-mile network of roads planned to extend all the way from Turkey to Singapore; a 32-nation, $1 billion Asian Development Bank; and the huge Mekong River Development Program.

The Thai government places major hope in the strength of regionalism to head off unwanted interference in its affairs by any of the great powers, including the United States. Foreign Minister Thanat Khoman recently told Drew Middleton of *The New York Times* that he believed Southeast Asia had the resources and would develop the political means to "balance" the weight of Communist China. He looked forward to an eventual grouping of Burma, Cambodia, Indonesia, Malaysia, the Philippines, Singapore, South Vietnam and Thailand. This grouping, he said, "will cooperate with the major powers—the United States, the Soviet Union and the Chinese — but it is not going to accept their dictation on issues that affect the members of the group."

The Thais are anxious, above all, to keep their national individuality and not be submerged by foreign influence. The topic is one of lively debate over cocktails in Bangkok and in academic monographs as well. In their headlong rush to modernization, will the Thai people hold on to traditional values? The merchandisers of consumer goods consistently put forward the virtues of possession — through billboards, press and cinema advertisements, radio and television commercials — and here, as in other parts of the world, the appeals are irresistible. There is a steadily increasing demand for luxury and "status" goods everywhere in Thailand, and a good many Thai intellectuals are worried about it. Sumat Jumsai na Ayutya, a brilliant Thai writer, regrets that his people "are concerned only with trying to catch up with the material side of Western progress, something which they will never be able to do, simply because it is part and parcel of the cultural West."

On the other hand, Thai scholar Phya Anuman Rajadhon believes that Thailand must change along with the world community because "we would perish if we tried to disassociate from it." But he warns against an indiscriminate borrowing of alien culture. The very fact that cultural differences are recognized and talked about in both East and West suggests that mankind has progressed a long way in the direction of mutual respect and good will. Too often in the course of history have relationships between the two major segments of the globe been soured by simple misunderstanding of the other fellow's philosophical point of departure.

Those who know this country best are generally of the opinion that Thailand's cultural borrowing will be selective, and not destructive of the national psyche. The tree-lined *klongs* of Bangkok may be giving way before the proliferation of Western-style buildings and traffic-choked streets. But the Thai people, cradled in freedom, tranquillized by Buddhism, and warmed by the tropic sun, have changed very little in the new era. This is still the land of *sanouk*. As former Thai Ambassador to the U.S. Sukich Nimmanheminda once observed to an American audience: "We turn to you for technical help, but not in the search for happiness. We would like to teach you the art of being happy." It might be the most valuable lesson to be learned by the Western world.

Bibliography

HISTORY

Chula Chakrabongse, H .R. H. Prince, *Lords of Life*. Taplinger, 1960.
Collins, Maurice, *Siamese White*. Faber & Faber, 1965.
Dhani Nivat, Kromamun Bidyalabh, H. H. Prince, *A History of Buddhism in Siam*. The Siam Society (Bangkok), 1965.
Griswold, A. B., *King Mongkut of Siam*. The Asia Society, 1961.
Moffat, Abbatt, *Mongkut, the King of Siam*. Cornell University Press, 1961.
Smith, Ronald B., *Siam, or the History of the Thais from Earliest Times to 1569 A.D*. Decatur, 1966.
Wan Waithayakon, H. R. H. Prince *(trans.)*, *Stone Inscriptions of Sukhothai*. The Siam Society (Bangkok), 1965.
Wood, W.A.R., *History of Siam*. Chalermnit Bookshop (Bangkok), 1959.

SOCIAL AND CULTURAL STUDIES

Anuman Rajadhon, Phya, *(trans*. William J. Gedney) *Life and Ritual in Old Siam*. Human Relations Area Files, 1961.
Ayer, Margaret, *Made in Thailand*. Knopf, 1964.
Coughlin, Richard, *Double Identity: The Chinese in Modern Thailand*. Oxford University Press, 1960.
De Young, John E. *Village Life in Modern Thailand*. University of California Press, 1958.
LeMay, Reginald Stuart, *A Concise History of Buddhist Art in Siam*. Tuttle, 1963.
Philipps, Herbert P., Thai Peasant Personality. University of California Press, 1965.
Skinner, George W., *Chinese Society in Thailand: An Analytical History*. Cornell University Press, 1957.
Skinner, George W., *Leadership and Power in the Chinese Community of Thailand*. Cornell University Press, 1958.
Thai Culture, New Series (23 vols. by various authors). The Fine Arts Department (Bangkok), 1962-63.
Wilson, David Allen, *Politics in Thailand*. Cornell University Press, 1962.

PICTURE BOOKS

Boulle, Pierre *(trans.* Gordon Graham; phot. Herbert Knapp),
　Walt Disney's Siam. Nouvelles Editions S. A. (Lausanne), 1958.
Hürlimann, Martin, *Bangkok.* Viking, 1963.
Nach, James *(ed.), Thailand in Pictures.* Sterling, 1964.
Wening, Rudolf and A. F. Somm *(phot.* Michael Wolgensinger),
　Thailand. Universe, 1961.

GENERAL

Audric, John, *Siam, Land of Temples.* Robert Hale, 1962.
Bartlett, Norman, *Land of the Lotus Eaters.* Jarrods, 1959.
Busch, Noel F., *Thailand, An Introduction to Modern Siam.*
　Van Nostrand, 1964.
Cripps, Francis, *The Far Province.* Hutchinson, 1965.
Damrong Rajanubhab, H.R.H. Prince, *Miscellaneous Articles*
　Written for the Journal of the Siam Society.
　The Siam Society (Bangkok) 1962.
Eyre, John D., *Thailand.* Ginn, 1964.
Felicitations Volumes of Southeast-Asian Studies (2 vols.).
　The Siam Society (Bangkok), 1965.
Harris, George L. and others, *Area Handbook for Thailand.*
　U. S. Government Printing Office, 1966.
Insor, D., *Thailand, a Political, Social and Economic Analysis.*
　Praeger, 1963.
The Journal of the Siam Society (1904-　　), Bangkok.
Pendelton, Robert L., *Thailand, Aspects of Landscape and Life.*
　Duell, Sloan & Pearce, 1962.
Perera, Walter, *(ed.), Thailand Year Book, 1966-67.*
　Temple Publicity Services (Bangkok).
Smith, Malcolm, *A Physician at the Court of Siam.*
　Country Life, 1947.
Thailand Official Year Book. Office of the
　Prime Minister (Bangkok).
Thompson, Virgina, *Thailand, the New Siam.* Macmillan, 1941.
Wood, W.A.R., *Consul in Paradise.* Souvenir, 1965.

Index

Credits

THAILAND TODAY was produced under the editorial supervision of Norton Wood. The book was designed by Albert Sherman. Picture editing was done by Mollie Cooper and picture layouts were prepared by John Woods.

The drawings that appear at chapter openings are the work of Ed Young.

The pictures appearing in the Color Portfolio beginning on page 89 were taken by the following photographers:

Page

89—Jerry Cooke

90, 91—Farrell Grehan

92, 93—Jerry Cooke

94, 95—C. A. Peterson, from Rapho Guillumette

96, 97—Harry Redl, for Silver Burdett

98—Rene Burri, from Magnum

99 through 103—Jerry Cooke

104—C. A. Peterson, from Rapho Guillumette

105—Rene Burri, from Magnum

106, 107—Jerry Cooke

108 through 111— Henry Clarke for *Vogue,* copyright © 1965 by The Condé Nast Publications, Inc.

Page

112, 113, 114—Jerry Cooke

115—Harry Redl, for Silver Burdett

116, 117—Jerry Cooke

118, 119—Rene Burri, from Magnum

120, 121—Jerry Cooke

122 through 125— James Pickerell, from Black Star

126, 127—Jerry Rose, from Pix

128, 129—Jerry Cooke

130, 131—Tor Eigland, from Black Star

132, 133—Jerry Cooke

134, 135, 136—Harry Redl, for Silver Burdett

DATE DUE